COURAGE &
CONFIDENCE

WHAT IT REALLY
TAKES TO SUCCEED
IN BUSINESS

EDITED BY PEACE MITCHELL & KATY GA

WOMEN CHANGING THE WORLD PRESS

Women Changing the World Press together with KMD Books acknowledges the Elders and Traditonal owners of country throughout Australia and their connection to lands, waters and communities. We pay our respect to Elders past, present and emerging and extend that respect to all Aboriginal and Islander peoples today. We honour more than sixty thousand years of Indigenous women's voices, stories, leadership, wisdom and love.

Edited by Chelsea Wilcox

Typeset in Adobe Garamond Pro 12/17pt

A catalogue record for this work is available from the National Library of Australia

National Library of Australia Catalogue-in-Publication data:
Courage & Confidence/Peace Mitchell and Katy Garner

ISBN: 978-0-6454374-0-9 (Paperback)
ISBN: 978-0-6454374-1-6 (Ebook)

Front cover design by redhotblue creative agency

This book is for our daughters and future generations of girls, may they have within them the courage and confidence to follow their dreams and know that they have the power to achieve anything they set their hearts on.

CONTENTS

FOREWORD
Amanda Thompson

ADVERSITY IS A GIVEN. COURAGE IS A CHOICE

It's hard in life to be brave and bold but we should never choose to be anything less. If life has taught me anything, it's that you have to live it with a lot of grit, determination and passion. You must take chances and give everything your all.

Some of the greatest life lessons can be learnt in nature. When it comes to triathlon, you are at the mercy of two opponents – the voice inside your head and mother nature.

An ocean swim in a triathlon is often shaped like a box. You have to swim straight out through the waves. Then you have to swim across the waves. Then when you reach the final buoy, you swim back in with the waves. As you are trying to swim out against the waves, sometimes you take one stroke forward and the wave pushes you ten strokes back. It's tiring and disheartening. But, unless you want to quit, you have no choice but to take on the waves – so that's what you do.

The waves in the ocean are like the challenges we face in life. They stand between us and success – us and the finish line. In life it can feel like we face challenge after challenge. As the saying goes: when it rains, it pours.

If at any time during the swim it becomes too much, you can put your hand up and in an instant it can all be over. No more waves. No more setbacks. No more challenges. If you put your hand up, if you give up during the swim, you will not be completing the remaining two legs of a triathlon – you will not be crossing the finish line.

I think the road to success is so often like that. The challenges we face are hard and giving up is easy. But if you give up, you'll never achieve the things you want to achieve in life. And you know what, maybe your next break is just around the corner. If you hold on, if you keep persevering to that final buoy out in the ocean, then the waves that have been your worst enemy become your best friend because you ride them into shore.

Peace and Katy's passion and commitment to women is infectious. We are blessed that they provide women with an inclusive and empowering environment to share, learn and celebrate. Being in business on your own is not an easy journey, and no matter what stage your business is in, this book will provide you with tools and mindsets to take on the waves and never give up. On behalf of all of us that need this book; thank you.

Remember, courage is being able to say, 'Not this and not now.' Confidence is knowing that you can take that first step forward with the strength of the stories and advice within this book.

AMANDA THOMPSON

Amanda renews personal and business confidence, teaching businesswomen the value of their services with the end goal of compensating themselves fairly. She provides the financial knowledge and confidence to have a great relationship with money and to become their own CFOs (confident, focused and on top of their finances).

In her course, Financially Fit Women, Amanda brings together her twenty years of financial advising and her life experiences. She always keeps her education and herself 'real' and is always available to discuss and support you in the areas that you fear. The name Endurance Financial stems from Amanda's passion of competing in Ironman Triathlons.

Instagram: endurancefinancial & amanda_tri_mum
LinkedIn: amandathompsonfp
Facebook: WomensFinancialFitness

INTRODUCTION
Peace Mitchell & Katy Garner

'All our dreams can come true if we have the courage to pursue them.'
– Walt Disney

I've always been a dreamer. Most people are. Having the dreams is rarely the problem. They know what they want. They know what their dreams are and how good it would feel to achieve them.

But why is it that so many women hold back from following their dreams? Why are so many women stopping themselves from playing bigger, from dreaming bigger or from allowing themselves to do all of the things that they want to do and know that they are capable of? Staying small serves no-one. It's not easier. It's not safer. It's not cheaper or more fun. And yet, so many women don't seem to have the confidence to step out and really go for their biggest dreams.

Having courage and confidence in yourself is an incredible force of power that starts with you. Whether you want to change the world, invent an innovative new product, take on the big brands, inspire people, take your business to the global stage or start a movement there's never been a better time to get started than right now.

This book is for anyone who knows there's more for her. Anyone who knows they have the power and potential inside them to achieve their goals and for anyone who knows that it's time to step out of their comfort zone, embrace their courage and confidence and start living the life of their dreams!

Written by twenty-four women who have learnt how to do it themselves, this book guides you through the steps to develop your courage and confidence and reach for your dreams whatever they may be. Combining inspirational stories and expert business advice, this book shares the life-changing power of what can happen when you learn how to let go of fear and activate your courage and confidence.

THIS BOOK CHANGES LIVES

Proceeds from the sale of *Courage and Confidence* go to providing marginalised women in business with scholarships to enable them to receive support, mentoring and education through The Women's Business School.

Aligning with the United Nations SDG goals for gender equality, The Women's Business School scholarships are awarded to women in remote and rural areas, Indigenous women, migrant women, survivors of domestic violence, women with disability and chronic illness and those facing financial hardship.

We believe that investing in women is the most powerful way to change the world and these scholarships provide opportunities for deserving women to participate in Ignite, a six-month incubator program for early-stage startups and businesses, and Accelerate, a six-month accelerator program for high potential and experienced entrepreneurs ready to scale their companies and expand globally.

Read more here: thewomensbusinessschool.com/scholarship

THE POWER OF BELIEF

Amy Huebner

When I was in my twenties, I overheard my mum say, 'Amy will land on her feet, she always does. I'm not worried about her.'

When I look back over my forty-odd years of existence, I have to agree, she wasn't wrong. At the time, however, it felt hard. Hard because of the pressure to meet those expectations Mum had of me. Hard because I felt I couldn't ask for help. Hard because it felt like failure wasn't an option.

It sure is lovely when others believe in you. What if your self-belief isn't as high?

If you are anything like me, it's easy to be hard on yourself. It's much harder to believe in yourself.

LOOKING IN THE MIRROR

I was working in the corporate world in Sydney, Australia, from a very young age. Expectations were high. When I stepped into the world of motherhood decades later, the pressure felt even greater.

I now had little humans to keep alive, for starters. It's not just about me anymore. Bundle this with the pressure to have your house in order, have your kids happy, healthy and thriving; and to provide a stable home – it's a lot! Throw work into the mix and our minds are running at warp speed.

How can we achieve all of this? CAN we achieve all of this?

Having lost my mum to cancer before I had my children, I have had to funnel the memory of her belief in me through to my own beliefs. As someone that apparently needs constant reassurance (thank you therapy) it's not easy to keep my mum's belief system alive. Especially when susceptible to being very self-critical. It is the memory of her, and the constant support of a handful of great friends, that provides the injection of reassurance that I look for, that I need to keep my own belief system on track.

When I had my children – three, in my case – energy reserves disappeared pretty quickly. Cue Netflix.

My needs often got lost in the process.

LEARNING TO SEPARATE MY CHILDREN'S NEEDS, MY DESIRE TO ENSURE THEIR NEEDS ARE MET AND MY OWN NEEDS IS ONE OF THE FIRST THINGS I NEEDED TO MASTER

Easier said than done. It can take a while to know where the parenting line stops and where our identity line begins.

The necessity to work is there for most of us. When it came down to it, I couldn't see how a traditional 'working for the man' job was going to fit in with the requirements of caring for my children. I also knew that I needed to have the stimulation of something outside of my family's needs. Or I would go nuts!

My future in business was on my mind every day as my children grew. For one, I was going to have to start bringing some money into the home if we were going to continue living where we were. My husband had a good job, however, with one income, we couldn't sustain our current living arrangements. I needed to start to contribute in a mone-tary way, and soon.

Considering how much we do as mothers, it is hard to imagine that we don't feel we are 'contributing' or able to see our great worth – mad-ness really, and yet, that is how a lot of us feel.

Yes, I had given birth, and boy, aren't we pure legends for doing this?! What about other skills? What else am I good at?

Prior to having my first child, I worked a contract to the end date so I had no job to return to. With varying business management skills, I knew my capabilities in those areas, but those types of roles are typically full-time and demanding. Living in a small town in country Victoria meant finding a flexible role in this line of work was unlikely.

That aside, in my former corporate roles, I often felt like I was 'creat-ing' work for the sake of having a role. Leaving me feeling like my work didn't matter in the grand scheme of things. I certainly didn't want to feel that way again if I could help it. My time away from the children is valuable. I wanted it to matter.

IT WAS TIME FOR ME TO DEFINE WHAT MY DESIRES AND NEEDS WERE

1. To bring in an income to help support my family.
2. Have a balanced work life so I can be present for my children.
3. Feel that I am contributing. To my family, as well as to others, in a positive way. I wanted to make a difference.

WHEN MUMMA BEAR RAISES HER HEAD

Whilst I was craving more adult interaction, I knew that I wanted to continue to be available to my children whenever I needed to be.

Growing up, independence was something that I needed to have, whether I wanted it or not. My mum and dad divorced when I was three, and my mum was a single mum trying to make ends meet for my brother and I. I was often left to my own devices for hours each day whilst my mum worked. I made my own way to and from school each day. It was a different time back then, so it was not uncommon for this to be the case.

I remember one time I got on the wrong train when coming home from ballet class. I had to get off and ask someone to help me find the right train home. I was over an hour late getting home and I was certain Mum would be so worried. When I got home, no-one was there. No-one was worried.

That amount of alone time and independence so young left me craving love and reassurance all my life. Still to this day. It has affected my relationships, my self-esteem, and of course, my belief in myself, and my belief that I matter.

I did not want this for my boys.

Now, it wasn't all bad! Forced independence from a young age made me very resilient, and frankly, less afraid to put myself out there. I travelled to many places around the globe on my own which allowed me to really value the differences in all of us. I learnt and appreciated that we all have our own strengths and weaknesses. On the whole, when we are trying our best, we can't go wrong. We may stumble, but that is part of learning. There is no road map to success, it looks different for all of us.

When it came time for me to look up from my babies and expand my responsibilities, I started looking for a road that meant I could keep my children – my *why* – in the frame, as well as fill my cup with purpose and fulfillment.

So how was I going to make that happen?

IF THE SYSTEM DOESN'T WORK FOR YOU, THEN IT IS TIME TO MAKE YOUR OWN SYSTEM

An opportunity came my way and almost immediately I felt an alignment with my goals. I didn't know how exactly, but I knew I needed to sit up and pay attention. There is a lot to be said for 'gut instinct'.

The opportunity in front of me was very new to me. However, if it ended up being the right fit for me, I knew I could make it work if I really wanted it to.

It meant starting my own business. Not something I ever thought I would do, and yet, a no-brainer at the time.

HOW TO BE 'NICHE' ABOUT IT

Ever heard the saying 'Jack of all trades, master of none'? Not the best reputation for a business owner to have.

Whilst it can be tempting to expand the range of your services, this is not always the best way to get noticed.

Becoming a known expert in your field can take time. A way to help this process is to narrow down the parameters of what it is that you offer.

WHAT IS YOUR NICHE?

When advertising your business and what it is that you do, the simpler your message, the better. Narrowing down your offerings can help potential customers find you – they'll know exactly what you offer, and therefore know if you offer something they want or don't want. Whilst this might mean you lose a broader audience, you gain more attention from an audience that matters. An audience made up of your ideal clients and customers.

Not only does having a niche help when it comes to marketing your business, it helps with your success rate and reputation. Finessing your skills and knowledge within a focused area can allow for greater success. Happy clients equal referrals. Word of mouth is a very powerful thing.

Having a niche can also help keep *the beast* at bay.

We can try to run away from imposter syndrome all we like; however, it tends to catch us at some point. Having a niche can help reduce these moments. Your experience and knowledge in your specalised area grows exponentially as time goes on, as does your belief in your offerings. See you later, imposter syndrome!

BOUNDARY FENCES

I would love to say that I only do the work that I want to do. I would also love to say that I know how to say NO when I feel I should. This is an area that I am still working on.

Working on our self-belief includes working on the belief that our time, and what we have to offer, is valuable.

I'm not sure any of us can avoid learning the lesson of being taken advantage of as a small business owner. It can take us a while to build up the courage to know our worth and value it. To believe in our expertise and stand by it. I was saying YES way too much and trying to please any-one and everyone. I was taking on too many tasks, as well as taking on the emotions of my clients. I was overwhelmed and not coping.

In addition, I soon learnt that babies and young children on workdays don't mix. When I tried juggling both, I found my mental health took a dive. The guilt I carried at the end of the day for being short-tempered with the children when they were interrupting me trying to work was terrible! I found myself starting to resent both my children and my clients. Not good!

I hit a wall.
I knew something was going to have to change.

Taking steps to set boundaries for yourself, and with clients, will not only help your ability to cope, it helps with productivity.

For myself, allocating child-free workdays allowed me to get a han-dle on things. I was able to be present for my clients and present for my children. Game changer.

For clients, I set expectations right from the beginning.

- Service inclusions.
- How and when they can contact me.
- How and when I will be contacting them.
- What the deliverables will be and when delivery is/service ends.

Setting boundaries and expectations can set a positive tone for your business. Having everyone on the same page builds confidence, helping to provide a great working relationship. The relationship you have with your client is one of your most valuable assets when it comes to good business.

BREATHE AND BELIEVE

It takes time to get into a rhythm with business. There are ebbs and flows. This can continue for years, possibly even the lifetime of a business. It can be hard to go through the ebbs. Doubt can understandably start to creep in. It's these times that you want to take stock. Breathe and believe.

A friend of mine came up with a great idea for moments of doubt.

AN 'EVIDENCE FILE'

Each time you get an awesome review, or a truly heartfelt email from a client thanking you for what you did for them, file it under 'E'.

When you find yourself having more downtime than you care for, or if that imposter monster is paying you an unwelcome visit, head on over to your evidence file. For me, this file goes a long way to filling that reassurance cup of mine.

On the flip side, downtime can be a positive. Use the time wisely.

- Set up/refine your systems. How can you streamline the steps of your customer or client process better?
- Design and schedule social media and other communication tasks i.e. newsletters, emails.
- Follow up with leads.
- Reach out to potential collaborators.

Amazingly, and before you know it, it'll be time for another flow. All the work you did during your downtime will make that flow a smoother journey.

> *TIP: Avoid dropping the marketing ball during busy times. Keeping your exposure high with constant communication with potential customers is what gets the 'flows' coming back each time.*

Is it still just an idea? Perhaps you are feeling ready to make a change?

Whatever your circumstances, if you are reading this book, particularly my chapter, then I am tipping it's time for you to sit down and think about those desires and needs of yours.

Maybe your desires and needs have changed and need to be redefined. Finding out what really matters to you can drive you to succeed. It's worth defining what that is.

I would like to think it was multiple factors that allowed me to succeed with my business, but when it came down to deciding to move ahead with it, the little girl in me didn't see failure as an option (thanks, Mum). Success is what I envisaged, and I truly believed in that vision. I feel that really made the difference to my journey.

The best way to keep your vision alive is to remain confident in your offerings, align with your ideal clients and let the others fall away, help reduce inevitable overwhelm by sticking to your boundaries and setting up efficient systems every chance you get, and most importantly, *believe in yourself* and what it is you can offer. Amazing things can happen.

I would like to leave you with a this …

> *'One of the most courageous things you can do is identify yourself, know who you are, what you believe in and where you want to go.'*
> *– Sheila Murray Bethel PhD, bestselling author*

AMY HUEBNER

As a certified sleep consultant, Amy Huebner founded Hushabye Baby in 2017. She specialises in newborn, infant and young children sleep, and works with families to provide them with tools and support to achieve great sleep for each member of the family. Amy lives in country Victoria with her husband and three young boys and works out of her home office in the family home. Having had her children throughout the time of building up her business, she knows all too well how difficult it can be juggling business pressures with raising a family. Amy is a big advocate of work-life balance and achieving personal success whilst also keeping a family's wellbeing in mind.

Amy has worked with over five hundred families, helping them sleep well and providing them with the education on how to keep great sleep a big part of their family life going forward. She hopes to continue to do this work for many years to come and is constantly looking to grow in the health and wellbeing space, in the hope of spreading knowledge on the vital necessity for a happy, healthy life: great sleep!

Website: hushabyebaby.com.au

BE THE HERO OF YOUR OWN STORY

Annette Densham

The walk home from school seems to take forever, especially as I watch the big black storm front build in front of us. One foot in front of the other. Every now and then, I put on a little speed, pull my little sister by her arm, urge her to walk faster. I clutch in my sweaty little hands – my most prized possession. I'm desperate to show Mum. In front of the entire school I had been presented the Top Dog Award for Achievement. I have never won anything before and am so proud.

This school is my third primary school in two years. I plod along doing my work, but I didn't think kids like me won anything. It is always the good-looking kids, the kids with both parents, the kids who live in the same house they came home to when they were born or the kids who can afford tuckshop every day. Not a kid like me. A kid without a dad. A kid with a stressed-out, freaked-out mum who cleans other people's houses to put food on the table. A kid so shy she hides behind her hair. Me.

As I push open the front screen door, it bangs on the wall behind it, making a huge crashing sound. Mum yells from the kitchen, 'For fuck's sake, be careful!' The little bundle of excitement and pride in my tummy dwindles just a little. *Great, Mum is in a cranky mood.* Walking into the kitchen, she's on her hands and knees washing the floor. Sweat from her brow, beaded like little drops of rain on the windows, makes her face shiny and red.

'Mummy, guess what?' my voice is high-pitched with excitement.

'What?' Mummy says. 'Hurry up. I've got to get this floor done.'

'Mummy, I won an award today.' If my chest could puff out any more, I would look like a big happy balloon. I hold out the yellow A4-size award with ACHIEVEMENT written in bold red letters.

'That's nice, Annie. Don't let it go to your head. No-one likes a show-off.'

Balloon deflated.

My mother's mindset was not her fault. She grew up in a time that didn't value women. She was repeating what her mother had taught her. Yet, her words cut me deeply as my little seven-year-old self came to terms with her unimportance in the world.

That moment. That statement. Those few words dictated how I would show up through my teens to my mid-forties. I hid. I didn't talk about myself out of fear that people wouldn't like me. I didn't do anything to stand out. I stopped sharing my stories – scared I would be shut down again. But when it came time to pick what I would do when I grew up, I chose journalism because I wanted to give people the opportunity to be heard, because if we rely on others for validation, we will always live in the shadows.

Fast-forward to the woman that little girl grew up into, she realised if she didn't put herself in the story and if she did not share her stories, it was not just her missing out. It is the same for anyone who is reluctant to share their story.

Stories are a gift that keeps on giving. When you tell stories – about your business or about you – you are connecting with others. Not just from a content point of view but from a physiological place. There is a science behind telling stories that goes beyond the business imperatives – connecting with your audience, building trust and being visible. Stories change people's brains. Reading or hearing a story lights up the receiver's brain like fireworks. Our bodies get off on stories, chemically and emotionally. Stories arouse our sensory cortex, activating so many parts of our brain and connecting our ideas, thoughts and experiences.

The question is why aren't you telling your stories?

If you had a similar experience to me, either knowingly or subconsciously, the message your soul heard is you are not good enough, you've not done enough, no-one is interested, or people think you are show-off, full of yourself or egotistical – it is not surprising you are keeping your stories to yourself. There are ways to work through these limiting self-beliefs to be the hero of your story.

And if you are in business, this reluctance to be the hero of your own story is hindering your growth and your ability to connect with your audience. They want to know you. People do business with people, not a logo or a snappy tagline or a slick website. They do business with *you*. The most cost-effective way to do marketing in your business is to get comfy with telling your story. It is a game changer.

SUCCESS IS AN INSIDE JOB

It's hard to be the hero of your own story if you battle doubt, fear, insecurities and imposter syndrome. Success starts and ends between the ears. When we go into business, all of those fears and doubts get magnified as we step out of our comfort zones. It is really easy to retreat and do what you feel comfortable with. That doesn't cut it in business. You HAVE to put yourself out there otherwise no-one knows you exist. If they do not know you exist, how can you sell to them? Building your confidence is a vital first step when you start your business – recognising the emotional and internal hurdles that will stop you from promoting what you do.

In 2013, my lovely, cushy, well-paying corporate job was made redundant. What started as an exciting opportunity ended less than twelve months later with a formal complaint against my manager and the loss of my job. I was crushed. It would not be an exaggeration to say I was devastated. I had recently returned to full-time work after being home with my kids for ten years. My confidence and belief in my abilities were like the shaky legs of a newborn giraffe. The treatment from my employer and the circumstances of my redundancy were seismic earth-shattering waves to my fragile ego. After months of not finding a job, I decided to start my own business. But I found there is a big difference between being skilled at a profession and running a business. I had no idea about so many things and the thought of promoting myself made me feel sick to the stomach. I knew if it was to work, it was up to me; no-one else was going to promote my business, so I enrolled in a twelve-month program that helped entrepreneurs work on their mindset and self-belief. It was a game changer.

If you struggle with putting yourself in the spotlight, think about hiring a coach, connecting with a mentor or seeking out a counsellor. Work through those barriers because they will hold back your business.

ACTION: Pick an aspect of yourself that you want to feel better about. Over the next month, at the end of every day, send yourself an email with a message written in third person about how awesome you are at something. Dear Annette. I admire the way you work through difficult times. You are so strong and brave. Love, Annette. Every morning, before starting your day, this is the message you will read. It will feel strange at first, awkward even, but the change in how you view yourself at the end of the month will blow you away.

EMBRACE YOUR GENIUS

I hadn't seen Jayne for a few months but had been following her online, watching her kick incredible goals in her business, winning awards and scaling her business. She'd taken her ecommerce business from a startup in her lounge room to a warehouse employing twenty-five people, turning over $5 million.

'Oh my goodness, you are kicking incredible goals. I am so proud of you,' I told her.

'Yeah, it's really nothing,' Jayne replied. 'I just do my thing.'

Her humbleness belied the massive accomplishments she had achieved, totally minimising the hard work and genius of her work into a few words – it is really nothing.

Um … so not true.

I was gobsmacked, but on reflection, I was not surprised. Far too many people in business – in life, for that matter – are so dismissive of their expertise and skills. This diminishing of our superpowers is pervasive across gender, race and cultural backgrounds. No-one is safe from the doubt that often clouds our most successful moments and the fear of being called out for being a show-off or bragger.

But there is no room for modesty in business. No-one else is going to promote you or market you. If you want your business to be in the spotlight, you have to get comfy with self-promotion. That means embracing your genius. It is not arrogant to own your superpowers. You have worked hard to get where you are, so own it. No-one else did the hard work for you. You did.

ACTION: Sometimes we need external validation of our awesomeness. Pick three friends who know you well and ask them what they love about you. You can do this by text or calling them. Take what they say about you and create a screensaver or write it on your bathroom mirror to remind yourself of your genius. You have skills, talents and a zone of genius that is worth acknowledging. After all, you didn't start and grow your business by being useless and talentless, did you? The success you have created comes from within you.

DITCH THE FRAUD FACTOR

Writing an award submission for a new client, I was trepidatious as I hit send. I was worried she wouldn't love it; I was scared she would think it was absolute crap and that I totally missed the heart of her business. A little voice in my head kept asking me who I thought I was.

You're kidding me, Annette. There are so many people better than you out there, inner voice tells me.

What do you mean? I've been doing this for years. I'm good at it, I argue back.

Really? Is that what you think? Pfft. You're a joke. She is going to hate it and wish she had picked someone else to do her submission, inner voice sneers at me.

Oh. Maybe you are right. There are so many others better than me, I cave into the voice.

When the email drops into my inbox, I open it with caution. Scared my client has worked out I am a complete fraud and have no idea what I am doing.

Dear Annette,

OMG. Wow! As I read this entry, I kept asking myself 'is this really me?' The person you have written about doesn't sound anything like me, but you have captured my story so beautifully. I cried when I got to the end of it because you made me sound so amazing. Thank you so much, you are such a talented writer.

Love, Katy

Okay. What's going on here? How can two accomplished, successful women in business be so uncertain of their skills and abilities?

It's called imposter syndrome and 70% of successful people suffer from it. *Suffer* is the right word. Imposter syndrome is when you doubt your abilities and feel like a fake. It leaves you questioning whether you deserve success, the accolades that come from achieving and if you have the abilities and skills to do what you say you can do. It is awful and is one of the biggest hurdles in being the hero of your own story. How can you soar when you have a chain of doubt holding you down?

> *ACTION: You can kick the FRAUD factor to the curb. There are five things you can do every day to build your inner hero. These tips are not a big secret. In fact, they are quite simple – but do not dismiss the power of simplicity. If you do these things every day, you WILL overcome feeling like an imposter.*

FESS UP

Talk, write and post about how you feel. You are not alone. Quite often, we live in our own heads and our brains do not know how to work out what is real and what is not. Even though you are incredibly talented and skilled (stop it, you are), when you tell yourself that you are not, your brain believes it. You are doing this to yourself. By acknowledging it is holding you back, you can take control. Like Uncle Ben told Peter Parker – with great power comes great responsibility. You have a responsibility to own your power so you can keep helping other people.

ADOPT A GROWTH MINDSET

The very clever Carol Dweck wrote a book called *Mindset* where she explores motivation and growth mindset. Those who hold onto the past, their failures and find it hard to embrace change, struggle with owning their achievements. Our brains are like plastic; we can change, and change comes with growing new neural connections and making existing ones stronger. But you have to want to change. If you change one thing about yourself, make it believing you are amazing.

SHUT UP

When that inner voice harps up and brings you down, physically get up and move. Shake your head and body and tell that voice to bugger off. It is a sad fact of life that the person we are most awful to is ourself. Would you talk the way you talk to yourself to your friend? No. So stop talking to yourself that way.

FACE THE FEAR

Standing on the edge of a diving board, looking down 200m into a swimming pool, my knees were knocking together. I was questioning why I had forked out $60 to do the southern hemisphere's tallest bungee jump. I was terrified of heights. Here I was with my ankles strapped together being encouraged to jump off a perfectly sturdy tower into that tiny pool of water. I turned to the guy and said … 'I can't do this. I think I am going to vomit.'

'Your choice,' he said nonchalantly, like he has heard this excuse from thousands of people. 'There are no refunds.'

I had just left my job, so I couldn't afford to lose $60 and not get value for money. I debated in my head what I had to lose, well, beside my life if the strap failed. Despite my overwhelming fear, I moved tentatively to the edge of the diving board.

'Don't look down,' the man said. 'Look out at the trees and pretend you are diving into a swimming pool to do laps. When you are ready, say one, two, three, fuck it and dive.'

So I did. As they pulled me from the pool, my heart pounding from adrenaline, I blurted … 'I want to do that again.'

I would never have had the experience if I had given into my fear. Now, that is an extreme example and if I hadn't done it, it wouldn't really have impacted my everyday life, but the rub is, so many of us run away from the things that scare us that *do* impact our everyday lives. When it comes to business, relationships and life in general, running away from our fears means we miss out on things and people miss out on what we can bring to their lives. Quite often the outcome is nowhere near as bad as what we made up in our heads. When it comes to business, being scared of doing Facebook Lives, Instagram Reels or making sales calls impacts the bottom line.

ACTION: Write down what scares you the most in business. Now you have in front of you, explore why that scares you. Dig deep – keep going until you have that aha moment.

Get some perspective:
- Are you really at risk?
- Will this kill you?
- If the worst was to happen, what would it be?

PERFECTION IS NOT YOUR FRIEND

One of the smartest men to ever live, Stephen Hawking, said, 'One of the basic rules of the universe is that nothing is perfect. Perfection simply doesn't exist … without imperfection, neither you nor I would exist.' Yet, so many strive for perfection when it is not possible. Nothing is perfect. Striving for perfection sets you up to fail right from the get-go. It is not the virtue you think it is. Perfectionism is not a sign of worth or success. It is not authentic. Perfectionists often live with discontentment and dissatisfaction because they never feel they're good enough. Striving for perfection leads to burnout, overwhelm and anxiety.

When you make a mistake or stuff up, the spiral into self-doubt and shame can be crippling. It is okay to fail. Failure is good – it is life's way of teaching us self-compassion and vulnerability. It opens up opportunities to take risks and makes us more resilient. If you are going to be the hero of your story, you have to show up authentically.

ACTION: Instead of striving for perfection, strive for excellence. Excellence is all about having high standards with the yoke of unattainable perfection. Having high standards leaves room for growth, improvement and quality. Whereas perfection leaves no room for mistakes, imperfections or compassion for self. Striving for excellence means you value the process, not just the outcome. Feel satisfied with a job well done and enjoy learning from your mistakes. At the end of each week, write down what you learnt and the expectations you placed on yourself. This will break the 'all or nothing' mindset. Write out the best/ worst/real scenario and aim for being real every time.

These tips won't help you tell your story, but they will help overcome what is stopping you from telling your story. Success is an inside job. If you can master what is going on between your ears, you will become a more authentic and vulnerable storyteller that people will want to hear from.

ANNETTE DENSHAM

With a gypsy as a mother, Annette Densham sought refuge in stories as her family moved from house to house. By the time she was seventeen she'd lived in ninety-six houses. The books in the library became her best friends and she immersed herself in tales of courageous heroes, incredible adventures and seeking knowledge about the world.

It was no surprise when she chose to go into journalism, the perfect career for her inquisitive and curious mind. After decades of writing – from major print publications and online magazines on topics from business and computers to seniors' issues and forklifts – she moved into corporate comms. Here she honed her storytelling skills, weaving words that moved people to tears, to give generously to worthy causes and to educate, empower and inspire.

Faced with the loss of her cushy corporate role in a 'financial restructure', she ventured out into entrepreneur land, eager to use her thirty-plus years in media to help people in small business. Working in public relations, she found a passion helping equip, educate and encourage businesses to use their stories to promote what they do across multiple channels.

Annette can't help but tell people's stories; it has been a huge part of her life. Working with professional businesses, she loves digging deep into their businesses to find out what makes them tick. Combining her skills as a journalist, her years in corporate comms and her ten years in PR, Annette's skill set is a canny combination that captures the many facets of a business. Coupled with her specialist skills as the queen of business awards, Annette can take a client from 'who are you?' to 'we want you' with her savvy outlook on building profiles and using content to drive organic reach.

Four-time recipient of the Grant Stevie Award for Women in Business, two-time winner of the Grand Stevie International Business Award, AusMumpreneur Author of the Year and PR World Awards PR Agency of the Year, Annette has definitely squashed the imposter in her head. Using all she has learnt about business and the inside work it takes to prosper, Annette's keynote Kick FRAUD Factor To The Kerb shines the light on how to overcome imposter syndrome.

Website: annettedensham.com
theaudaciousagency.com

NGALIMI YUNGGUDYA*
Applying an Indigenous Lens of Reciprocity
Bianca F Stawiarski

'A healthy Indigenous business model is based on reciprocity. If we treat business the same way we treat the land, we maintain balance. You must nurture a relationship and give something to it before you can take from it. It's all about relationships and balance.'
– A Burke, personal communication (November 2021)

Reciprocity is possibly the last thing that many people consider when starting on their entrepreneurial journey. Commonly the focus and priority are on profit and loss, business structure, ideal client and marketing – to name a few. While these are all important in operating a successful business, there is a growing social enterprise movement worldwide which considers ways of operating a business while facilitating a positive impact for the community and environment. Although there are some similarities, this chapter is not focusing on social enterprise, but rather exploring how reciprocity is viewed and practiced through an Indigenous** lens. This effectively decolonises and indigenises entrepreneurial approaches, recognising that our way of 'doing' business at the very core has always included reciprocity, balance and community for tens of thousands of years. Before you continue, please note that this is in no way suggesting that all First Nations peoples view the

---

*   Ngalimi yunggudya means we give to each other in Badimia/Badimaya language
**   The term Indigenous will be used interchangeably with First Nations

world in the same way; that would be disrespectful to the incredible diversity and uniqueness of First Nations peoples around the world. As a Badimia (Badimaya) woman, sovereign business owner and entrepreneur, this is from my own viewpoint. I ask that you remain curious and consider the benefits of embedding reciprocity within your business structure and operations. Even though it can be challenging starting or operating a business, I know within my very being that these five tips will help you bring heart, honouring and balance throughout your entrepreneurial journey.

TIP 1: HONOUR YOUR ANCESTORS

We are held on the shoulders of generations of strong men and women to be where we are today. Although this may sound cliché, our ancestors form the roots and foundation of our tree; they describe where we have come from, including who and what contributes to make up the person we are today. Our Ancestors give us strength, insight, connection and grounding, but likely also have passed on traumatic experiences from previous generations. A simple calculation shows that for any of us to be here, managing a business, even if we only considered ten generations, then an incredible 1,022 ancestors have come before us! Each of those 1,022 ancestors have overcome challenges, trauma and tragedy, survived against the odds, some have travelled the world, spoken different languages, developed skills, continued traditions or created new ones. Despite all the odds and probably many in less positive circumstances, your ancestors throughout the generations met and birthed the next generation. This may seem a foreign approach in business, but for Indigenous peoples, understanding and placing who we are, how we fit into interconnected relationships and the gratitude for those who come before us and those that are yet to come, becomes our foundation, our place of strength.

Ever considered how your ancestral roots lend you strength in your day-to-day life? It's an interesting thought, isn't it? It's worthy spending some time exploring what values you bring to the way you operate your business and where these may have come from. Likely your ancestors have contributed to or instilled these values within your very being, gifting them to future generations, and these have become integral to both you and the foundations of your business. Imagine if you lived your life and conducted your business as though your ancestors were standing beside you, supporting you and cheering you on!

How do we honour our Ancestors? The simplest way is to acknowledge, name and express your gratitude for them coming before you. Even if you don't know their names, respectfully thanking them for being the reason you are here today, including operating a business which hopefully improves other's lives through the products/services that you provide, is a starting place.

Even just one generation ago, a Ukrainian catholic man born in a displaced persons camp in Germany during post World War II, met a Badimia (Badimaya) woman, a single mother, herself a child of her own mother's life growing up in a catholic orphanage in Western Australia. Despite the differences in backgrounds, languages and countries of origin, they met and married in South Australia, and I was born. I learned many things from them both, all of which are integral to both myself and my business – determination and drive from my father, and relational connectedness and insight from my mother. Then there is my love of horses, who are involved in my business, that comes from my maternal great-grandmother, my love of the land from my paternal grandmother and my connection to Country through my maternal line. To not acknowledge my ancestors' roles in the person I am and the way I approach business ignores the roots of my tree, my very foundations, and for them I am grateful. Although it may seem a foreign concept, consider how could you express your gratitude for and honour your ancestors, their impact on your life and entrepreneurial activities?

TIP 2: DEVELOPING RESPECTFUL, TRUSTING RELATIONSHIPS WITH INTEGRITY

'Mainstream business models often see buyers and sellers transaction at arm's length, in a supply chain where participants never meet, and without developing the trust necessary to ensure an ongoing relationship.'
— *Associate Professor Bronwen Dalton, (2019)*

Respectful, reciprocal relationships incorporating *ngalimi yunggudya* are one of the cornerstones of Indigenous ways of doing business. As alluded to earlier, there is also a growing movement to include these types of relationships in non-Indigenous businesses globally through the social enterprise movement. This is certainly a move away from mainstream business models where the focus is on increasing use of automation and distance that may not feel relational in the sales and marketing processes, which essentially removes the development of trusting relationships. Please note that I in no way suggest that automation in business is something to be avoided. I actually use automation processes myself in a number of parts of my business, but there needs to be, at its core, a relationship of trust developed during and throughout the process on an ongoing basis. We also see this in the western concept of boundaries, specifically in the allied health space that I operate in. How can someone trust you with their pain, shame and/or fear if they know nothing of who you are as a person, your experiences and your values? Indeed, if you reflect, you may discover fond memories of a local corner store, or that small regional business where you are known both by name and what your favourite items are, compared to your experience of purchasing from a big business that doesn't know the first thing about you. This gives some insight into the importance of developing relationships. Indigenous businesses prioritise relationships and connection. We don't just know who you are and what you like to buy … we know your family and how you may relate to us, amongst many other things. I'm known for having a cuppa with clients or their families, sharing food, having a yarn, the biggest belly laughs or connecting people to others. This can be described through what Professor Judy Atkinson calls our 'community of care', which recognises diversity and support within community (Atkinson, 2019, 17).

I also value reciprocity between small businesses. I do this by purchasing from and supporting other small businesses, specifically Indigenous and/or female entrepreneurs that share similar values to my own. At times, I gift or discount services to people who need them but may not be in a position to pay for them, and I go out of my way to support people – it is the giving without expectation to receive where trust and relationship start to be formed. A client explained one of the reasons for being interested to engage with us and for continuing to access our services was that, 'There's never been a safe space in relationship for us to explore who we might be … you hold space in such a large way, including the earth and elements and nature and the animal beings,' (name withheld). A business built on relationships, through trust and integrity can generate an amazing movement of support, reciprocity and safety, instilling the values of *gudu-guduwa* (coming together) into the foundations of everything you do. The importance of relationship in business shows a growing, 'Need to move away from a transactional way of engagement to a relational way of engagement,' (Jarrett, 2019).

TIP 3: MAINTAINING AND CREATING BALANCE

Now that we've explored how Ancestors and relationships form the basis of *ngalimi yunggudya*, we need to consider how we maintain balance – both personally and professionally. This is possibly the most important tip, even though I've put it as number three, which underpins First Nations' approaches around the world. When we look at balance, we need to consider the interconnecting facets of how we as individuals, communities and entrepreneurs holistically approach this. We need to include mental, physical, emotional, cultural and spiritual (including connection to Country) aspects, all of which contribute to balance. 'Indigenous knowledge tells us that individual balance is intricately bound to interconnection with one's immediate family, extended family, one's community and one's relationship with the world at large, both natural and spiritual,' (First Nations Pedagogy Online). How then do we maintain balance as an entrepreneur? It is more than standard business processes, and far more than recognising that we need self-care as a form of bringing equilibrium. We need to consider how our actions and entrepreneurial approach impacts not just ourselves, but also the land, the community and both our ancestors and the ancestors of the Country that we are living on. We need to hold a form of ongoing ceremony, where every part of the entrepreneurial process honours, respects and gives first – understanding that this balance encourages flow and reciprocity. One way I do this is by recognising that as a Badimia (Badimaya) woman I am a visitor to Kaurna Country, even though I own a small farm here. I respectfully involve Kaurna elders in my services in a paid capacity, hearing the history of spirituality of this land through their knowledgeable voices as custodians. I also sought permission of Kaurna elders to operate my business on their land as a respectful way of honouring. This approach of maintaining balance goes into greater depth in the next two tips.

TIP 4: HONOURING, RESTORING AND CARING FOR THE LAND — WHY WE MUST GIVE BACK

Continuing from the theme of balance, *ngalimi yunggudya* encompasses the importance of honouring the *barna* (land/Country) that we are on, including the ancestors that are singing within *barna*. I can almost hear you ask, *What does giving back to the land have to do with business?* We respect and honour the land, caring for the wild spaces, including the animal and plant beings, as well as nurturing the places that have been hurt. On our sanctuary in the north-east Adelaide Hills, we have both created natural spaces for healing and encouraged other spaces to return to tangled bush growth rather than farmland. We have planted many local native plant species, constructed bird boxes and protected nesting hollows in old trees. We greet the old grandmother tree like family and marvel in the life both of her and living within her boughs. Every visitor or client that comes to our sanctuary eventually meets the grandmother tree, introducing themselves and listening for her response. They see her scars from many, many bush fires, and resonate with experiences of hurt. *Barna* heals and regulates. By caring for *barna*, we are in turn cared for and nurtured. How can you involve honouring the land in your business? Even if your business is a warehouse, what can you do that recognises the ancestors in the land – even if they are under slabs of concrete? In my case, the respect that we give to *barna* draws people to want to heal in those natural spaces and makes it a glorious, connected place to be. We give to the land and the land gives to us. Finally, one further area of *ngalimi yunggudya* is giving back to community, which leads us on to our final tip.

TIP 5: COMMUNITY OBLIGATIONS, INCLUDING THE IMPORTANCE OF GIVING BACK

Here we are … our final tip! *Ngalimi yunggudya* must involve both recognising community obligations and appropriately giving back to your local and wider communities. As has been highlighted throughout this chapter, the principle of reciprocity is that we must give before we can receive. Importantly, giving without an expectation of receiving! So how do you, as a business owner, meet community obligations? What are your skills and expertise? I do this in a few ways. As a coach and therapist, I support members of the community as they need it or utilise my networks to extend the level of support. In many cases, I do this pro-bono or as part of a barter system. I also volunteer coordinate Indigenous business networking events, and I help businesses navigate the startup phase. Other ways of giving back are through purchasing products/services from other small businesses, either Indigenous small businesses or female entrepreneurs. I share their content, services or products on my business pages or promote them to other people that may benefit from them. I know that I am both expected to support community AND am honoured to provide support in various ways. Another way that I help community is through giving First Nations people an opportunity for employment, training or volunteering opportunities. What could you do for your community? How do you give back?

Throughout this chapter we have explored reciprocity, or *ngalimi yunggudya,* through a First Nations lens. We have considered how we can honour our Ancestors, enter respectful relationships, maintain balance holistically, while caring for *barna* and supporting community. We have shown how entrepreneurs can include these approaches in their company standard operating procedures, and how these may foster healthy, balanced businesses. *Ngalimi yunggudya* is the way First Nations people and businesses support positive, holistic and reciprocal relationships. When you consider all the benefits, what's stopping you?

REFERENCES

- J Atkinson. (2002 & 2019) *Trauma trails: Recreating song lines, the transgenerational effects of trauma in indigenous Australia.* Spinifex Press Pty Ltd Victoria
- *Holistic Balance Overview from the First Nations Pedagogy Online Project,* firstnationspedagogy.ca/holistic.html
- L Schubert. *What Mainstream Business Can Learn from Indigenous Business.* University of Technology, Sydney uts.edu.au/news/business-law/what-mainstream-business-can-learn-indigenous-business?

BIANCA F STAWIARSKI

Bianca Stawiarski is the founder and managing director of Warida Wholistic Wellness. She is a strong Badimia (Badimaya) woman, who is a centred and purpose-driven healer, consultant, speaker, lecturer, author, trainer and change-maker. Bianca infuses her calming, resilient, earthy, Indigenous connectedness into all that she does. As well as the work she does on Country, Bianca is sought out by organisations, companies and publications from right across the globe. She is a certified mental health practitioner with an interest in supporting people who have experienced complex trauma, and holds a master's in counselling practice, a Diploma of Life Coaching, Post Grad Diploma of Counselling, Certificate in Equine Assisted Psychotherapy and a Bachelor of Aboriginal Studies, amongst other qualifications. She is also currently undertaking a PhD in exploring whether the Indigenous healing practice of *dadirri* can assist people with dissociative identity disorder create inner communities of care. Bianca hopes the results can benefit some of our world's most disadvantaged and vulnerable people.

Her work has been recognised over the years; one recognition of note was winning the 2021 Global Business Mothers Awards in the Women Will Change the World and Oceania Business Excellence categories. This has encouraged her to reach further afield, providing online services and virtual coaching programs in therapeutic approaches, business support and personal development so that women, especially, have access to holistic specialist support regardless of where they live.

Warida Wholistic Wellness was borne through recognising that communities needed something different to western clinical approaches to improve the growing mental health crisis around the world. Bianca brought western clinical qualifications with Indigenous healing practices together, which included connection to Country. Warida became a sanctuary for wellbeing on Kaurna Country in the Adelaide Hills, Australia, where they provide the tools and support to create community change – one person at a time. At Warida, they get outside of four walls to connect to Country, animals and ourselves.

Whether it be working with Warida's horses through equine-assisted therapy, taking a walk on Country with bush therapy, yarning circles or drawing upon the natural wisdom of the grandmother tree, they love to take an intuitive and holistic approach. For those who can't attend their sanctuary, they created unique online one-to-one and work-at-your-own-pace coaching programs.

Warida Wholistic Wellness' purpose is to support the creation of strong empowered families, workplaces, services and communities, and to break through intergenerational trauma, disconnection and disempowerment. They also go one step further and provide volunteering, training and employment opportunities, and facilitate positive mental wellbeing and self-care practices in Australian First Nations people impacted by trauma. Their unique services are culturally safe, empowering and trauma informed. They are proud to be a Supply Nation Certified & Social Traders Certified Indigenous Social Enterprise operating at an international level.

Website: warida.com.au

GROWTH CAN STILL HAPPEN IN A PAUSE

Cath Nolan

The tiny ballerina's hand was a sticker on my kitchen floor. An elegant, white hand on a white background, almost blending in on that pale timber floor. For six whole frenetic, chaos-fuelled months, she stayed strong. Just her hand. It was like she was mocking me. Waving every time I rushed past. Her unspoken message screaming, *Honey, when are you going to get your crap together and get back on track?* That disembodied hand was a representation of ALL the little things I wasn't doing right.

To some, this might not be a big deal. But for me? I'm a Virgo. Tidiness is like oxygen. I need it to breathe.

Honestly, the ballerina sticker would have been easier to live with if she'd been giving me the finger. The politeness of her hand-wave gesture seemed to make it worse.

At the time, I felt like my life was on hold, my ambitions and dreams relegated to below the washing, the cooking, the playgroup and play dates and queue of highly nutritious lunch boxes, repeated daily.

I've had a few pauses on my journey. The biggest were kids, trauma and PTSD. Each pause took a debilitating toll on my courage – even those that were my choice. But with each pause, I've learned more.

I've learned how to feel better about taking time out from goal-achieving. And I've learned there are some actions that will ensure you actually keep growing forward, no matter what your ultimate goal is.

It's quite possible that my 'keep wining while you rest' advice is simply high-performer justification for pausing. But, well, whatever! The idea allows me to give in to rest, so maybe it'll do the same for you.

Pausing is essential. Like sleep or think time. But for those with big goals and big hearts, a pause can feel like failure.

If you have a huge dream or simply a passion to find one, you, my friend, will have ideas storming you like the front row of the Boxing Day sales shoppers at 9am on 26 December. Every time you're online, anytime you try to sleep, each shower. Your mind is popping with possibilities.

A pause allows you to reflect, to check back in with what's most important and what you've done well; to regenerate from going too fast or tangentially, and to reset.

But the pause only works magic for you if you allow it to. And if you're in the habit of resisting the pause, you're missing the benefit.

WHY WE RESIST THE PAUSE

Friend, your priority list is full, and your goals are big. You're naturally going to resist the pause the same way you'd resist anything that looks like keeping you from your goals. But the most disturbing part of a pause is often GUILT!

Not only do you expect to have accomplished more, you feel guilty for not enjoying what you HAVE achieved. But humans are complex – it's possible to feel joy and grief in the same moment. Like:

Yay I'm looking after my heart's purpose! But ughh, dark night of the soul, what I was doing no longer fits who I am and what I'm heading for hasn't started yet so I'm stuck here in this … this pause.

Hitting pause on your goals can happen for a bunch of reasons:

- Health. This was me – hello, complex PTSD. This is still me some days.
- Work. I've been at the coal face with hundreds who've experienced redundancy and career change.
- Life stage. You know, you've been on a path your whole life, reached success and suddenly realise it's meaningless and you've been chasing someone else's dream? So, you hit pause, either actively or mentally, while you figure things out.
- Caring reasons. Also me. This is the parents, the sons and daughters, siblings and good mates.

SECRET # 1 – REFRAME YOUR PAUSE

Calling it a pause sounds so orderly and planned, doesn't it? But living through it can feel like you're stuck in a stinking cesspit of stagnation. Frustration for weeks or months at a time. Or even longer.

You may not even have noticed the exact moment when you transitioned from joy to stagnation, but you recognise it when you've arrived. You're not flourishing. You feel annoyed, maybe a lot. Maybe you're more irrational, emotional or distanced than you usually would be. You're not growing or building.

Only: you are, my friend. In this exact moment, if you're paying attention, you can be growing. It's been this way for my coaching clients, for my friends and for me, personally.

The first time I was in a pause, it was the career kind. The level of discomfort was around six out of ten. Not extreme, but consistent. I loved the team I worked with – and half of my job was super satisfying. But like a stone in my shoe, the other parts of my job were causing a blistery, festy hot mess. For me it was the sales and the boys' club. Not everyone who worked there had the same experience, either. There are so many reasons you stay in a role past it's due date.

39

My husband gave me the courage to quit. And what I learned in that painful struggle to find a way to my next normal, came to be the basis of my work with others, for years to come.

But my second pause was much harder. A definite dark night of the soul and one I did not see coming. It was a spiral from subtle coercive control to all types of abuse. The experts who supported me said it was the worst case of psychological abuse they'd seen.

I felt utterly incompetent and completely stuck. At one point, I was suicidal. I truly believed this person I'd been so close to – believed that my family, my children and my friends – would be better off without me alive.

This seems like an awful story to tell you in an uplifting, motivating book. But I want you to know that success stories are not all roses-only journeys. That whatever is causing you pause has lessons for you. And that great success can be on the other side.

Finding a way to *own your story*, to own whatever has caused you pause, could well be that competitive advantage you've been looking for.

You know that feeling, when you hear someone super inspiring and you think, *Well, it's okay for them, with their connections, their brilliant team, their four nannies, perfect hair and supportive partner.* Like, happy for them really – but at the same time there's a whole emergency response team hosing down your own fire of confidence. Because without the perfect hair, perfect team, fab connections, who am I to think I can make it?

We're naturally wired to see our faults, and to assume everyone else sees them too. It's your egocentric bias.

So, if you're in a pause, contemplating a pause, or feeling like your dreams *are forever away*, this is for you. I stand with my hands on your shoulders, looking you in the eye since we've been friends forever.

Lovely, for you to get to where you want to be, I need you to know two things:

1. First, the pause ends. NEVER as fast as you'd like, but it ends and then there's sunshine.

2. Second, you'll learn your point of difference in the pause. Your advantage. Your fire, your strength.

In hindsight, each of my pauses have been the precise moments of mega-growth. Failure is the greatest teacher, right?

Right out of uni, I went to work for Flight Centre. Within the first year I accidentally sent a beautiful young couple to Vietnam without the appropriate visas. They got to Hanoi airport and were turned around. It cost them a lot of angst, time and missed opportunity. It cost Flight Centre over $20 thousand and I was sure it was going to cost me my job. But when the HR director sat me down, he said, 'That's the most expensive training you'll ever do. No way are you making that mistake again. Why would I give you the boot now?'

SECRET #2 – LOOK FOR THE LESSON

Let me tell you another story.

There's a guy sitting on his verandah with his dog and his mate. The dog is whining. The mate asks, 'What's wrong with your dog?'

The guy says, 'I think he's sitting on a nail.'

The mate's confused – 'Why doesn't he get off?'

And the guy says, 'I guess it doesn't bother him that much.'

The thing about pauses is that they're not always super obvious. You might experience it as a period of extra whining.

Of course, we all have issues that warrant a rant. But is there an issue you're complaining about consistently? Listen closely. This is where you can find the lesson and grow.

Pay attention to what you're whining about. Consistent complaints have lessons for you.

It's possible that you're already aware of what's bothering you and you'll get around to changing that or moving away from that eventually. But my question for you is why would you wait? Why would you tolerate less than incredible, for this one life you have?

SECRET #3 — SELF-CARE IS RUBBISH

How great would it be to feel like you were living your purpose? Creating the change you want to see in the world. That you had time for those you love, simply for fun or when they need you. That you had the money to see the world or upgrade to the car you REALLY want, without stress.

How great would it be to know for sure that your winning days at the grindstone are LEADING TO SOMETHING BIGGER for you? And that the tough days are NOT an indicator of the way things will be. To know your side-hustle has legs, or that you're not trapped under a toxic boss or a never-ending change cycle.

It's possible, but nobody feels the winning spirit constantly. Life is tough in some places where it should be joyous. Fear over your finances, disappointment that you can't give what you want, or that there's not enough left for YOU to do something fun, FOR YOU.

When your heart is heavy, self-care is often the first prescription you'll get from every well-meaning person who loves you.

But if you have a big dream you're chasing, this suggestion can make you want to punch someone. Or run away fast. Or stare dumbly, transfixed and mouth hanging open, at how little they know you.

SECRET #4 — YOUR GOALS ARE THE MAIN OBSTACLE TO YOUR GOALS

You know the number one thing getting in the way of you achieving your goals? It's your other goals.

So, you want to be the Insta-worthy wellness guru who's also a ferociously successful business mogul? And you have young kids and want to be present for every possible occasion. You can do anything you want, but you have to choose a priority. Or at least a few, cleverly aligned priorities.

For high achievers and big dreamers, this is where self-care sits. You see the great logical benefits, but at a core level, it conflicts with everything else you're striving for. It conflicts with all your other priorities.

I know this because I lived this. Then I found a strategy that was super simple, but it went deeper. It worked so well for my kids and me personally, that I used it with hundreds of my clients. Then thousands. They used it too and said they loved it. Then I wrote it into a book and it became an Amazon number one bestseller in under three hours.

In my experience, self-care is not the answer. Pedicures were buried on that never-get-to part of my to-do list, making me feel worse about my ability to accomplish things. Like the ballerina's hand – a constant reminder that I wasn't following the script. And gratitude – it works for some, but for me it was the WORST of the self-care options.

SECRET #5 – GRATITUDE KEPT ME SMALL

Gratitude kept me in an unsafe situation way beyond the smart departure time. I see the same play out for many of my clients. It's disempowering and needs a shift. I'll get to that.

Let me tell you a story. I was sensible, intelligent, educated. A Sydney girl with still-married, still-in-love parents. I'd worked hard and smart and I had the share portfolio, the property and the savings. I'd morphed my corporate career into a successful business, helping others to find their path and their courage.

But outside work, things were shifting dramatically. My life was threatened. My financial security vanished – all my savings, all my sensibleness. My inner good girl gave too much, and I became completely vulnerable. Clinging to gratitude and patience, but actually tolerating what I shouldn't have. It went too far. Without financial security, I had no options.

What felt like overnight, I became one of the invisible homeless, with nothing but my kids. My confidence was obliterated.

I learned how FAST a girl can go from having it all to having nothing. And that clear directions out of trouble mean nothing if you don't have the courage to take them.

I searched for answers. I'm a coach, so I had some problem-solving to draw on. But it wasn't enough – I needed DEEPER, BIGGER ANSWERS. I searched everywhere for resilience and courage advice, and was really disappointed.

Most of the suggestions you hear for building courage are fine if you're already flying and you just need a little 10% lift. But what about when someone's dealing with trauma from a workplace or at home? Or if you're so logistically BURIED, that you can't imagine how to get unstuck to do a great job NOW, let alone stretch to something bigger?

I'm sharing my story to show you, it is possible. I'm proof it's possible.

SECRET #6 – *THE DID GREAT HABIT*

My desk right now is a small antique pine Scottish farmhouse dining table. It's about as long as most dining tables are wide, with a drawer at one end with a pretty clear crystal knob.

After a few months as the invisible homeless, I'd gathered some money and was renting a house with my kids. But trauma chased us relentlessly. My vision for recreating a home filled with joy and laughter was slow to realise. There was nothing but stress in our household. The kids constantly bickering and angry; I felt permanently out-of-character fragile.

My pretty desk – small even as a desk – was our dining table. The kids were little, so we still fit. One quiet Wednesday, I sat in desperation with a stack of brightly coloured sticky notes, a short stubby grey vase and advice from my mum: 'Catch them being good, Cath.'

Between my dark night of the soul, endless pause, broken state, and their out of character bad behaviour, this was a stretch of all my creativity. But I wrote out five notes for each of them. Each note contained a thing they'd done that was great. These things were TINY, but it didn't matter. The vase of notes sat on the table all through dinner. They could barely look away, intrigued. At the end of dinner, we moved the plates to one side and read the notes aloud.

The kids were transfixed. Not just that, WE were fixed. Literally overnight, they stopped the bickering and started back to their old, thoughtful selves. Within twenty-four hours they were writing Post-it notes for each other and within seventy-two hours, they were writing what I had done that was great!

The Did Great Habit transformed our world. Professionally, it became a bestselling book and helped thousands of clients. Personally, this habit transformed my pause and gave me back a sense of control.

It gave me a constant little trickle of evidence that I was on track, that I was doing great. A constant reminder that I was capable of good things and achieving good things. Confident that when the time was right, I was able to be where I wanted to be.

WHAT NOW?

I have three questions to leave you with:

1. What are you whining about and how can you move away from it?
2. What are you great at and how can you leverage it?
3. What action can you take right now, to move you forward even a little? *Even if it's sleep!*

See, WHO YOU ARE, with your EXACT life circumstances and your unique, maybe even underrated experience, is EXACTLY who you need to be, to take that next step and have more for yourself.

You don't always need to FEEL on track, to be on track. The right next step isn't always clear, but *The Did Great Habit* will always serve you well and give you positive momentum. It triggers the brain. Reminds us – me, my kids and my clients – and you too, that we're capable of great things. And not just because we're lucky.

CATH NOLAN

A social entrepreneur with a mission to create real change, Cath is the founder of Gender Gap Gone and the Don't be ARSD Movement. A People's Choice Award-winning coach, her client list has included HP, Uber, Toyota, Disney, Johnson & Johnson, all levels of government and over six thousand individuals.

Three-time number one bestselling author and global keynote speaker on courage, leadership and inclusion, in 2021 Catherine won the prestigious AusMumpreneur Women Will Change the World Award. Combining her twenty years of coaching, and her experience as a single mum and trauma survivor, she helps people to achieve what they hadn't dared to dream was possible.

Find her on LinkedIn or on her website.

Website: cathnolan.com

LIVING A LIFE WITH PURPOSE

Chelsea Munro

When the sun rises, I throw the covers back, my feet hit the floor and I am thankful.

It wasn't always that way.

It was 2010, I was a single mum, juggling a senior sales career, working across three states with a beautiful, happy, healthy and well-adjusted nine-year-old girl.

Then she fell sick.

A sudden illness, eventually diagnosed as an appendicitis. The routine operation a success, but it was the weeks, that turned into months, that followed that truly tested every part of our being.

Grace developed a rare form of septicaemia, not seen in a child in Australia and that had an almost non-existent survival rate.

Culminating in twenty-three operations – with nineteen of those in twenty-one days – the most significant and enduring of those days came on 21 July.

Her tiny body ravaged with infection, she flatlined.

Life support, induced coma, renal failure and further cardiac arrest followed.

Every parent's worst nightmare.

To the doctors, surgeons, nurses and hospital staff that played a role in Grace's survival I will be forever thankful.

Six weeks later, she came home.

She is amazing, Grace and her little brother are my greatest loves and achievements but that is another story with many chapters.

It was a horrendous time in our lives that produced insurmountable pain, but it was not a wholly negative experience for us.

From that day forward, life was different.

That's the thing about trauma, you are thrust into this shit fight and spat out the other side, battered, bruised, shaken and smothered in anxiety.

There is no denying that this was the single most critical and significant series of moments that changed my life. Indefinitely.

I decided that kindness, appreciation and positivity would reign supreme and that I would practice being grateful every single day.

I found that the more blessed and grateful I was, the happier and healthier I became.

I didn't escape hardship, in fact, the years that followed saw family breakdown, IVF, death, the end of a long-term relationship, and being from the land, the survival of one of the worst droughts in history.

Through it all, I practiced happiness.

It was never a case of, 'Gee, she's lucky,' or the flip side of that, 'Gee, she works so hard,' it was, in fact, a very simple choice.

Every single day I choose happy.

I wake up and I am happy, whatever shitshow that may develop can often be beyond my control, but at that very first moment of my feet hitting the floor, I am happy.

It is a choice.

I choose to live my life with purpose.

Research tells us that by adapting to this way of life, we will be healthier, live a longer life and be more psychologically resilient.

We can all have a purpose, or a reason why we do/how we do or why we live by it. However, to fully achieve this we need to truly align with our core values, strengths and beliefs. We need to integrate passion and purpose, ensure our daily decisions influence our habits and behaviour along with shaping our goals to encourage focus and self-belief.

And when that alignment occurs, be ready for the magic.

Sounds great, but is it really just thinking happy? No. It's making daily clear and conscious decisions to impact what you want to achieve.

We often hear people say they want a car, they want a holiday, they want to move, but it takes positive action to make that happen. Wanting a car won't happen if you don't put the funds aside and save for the vehicle. Wanting is not enough.

Living a life with purpose takes practise daily, I encourage you to text a friend you haven't spoken to in a while, buy some flowers for yourself or someone special, shout a coffee to the stranger behind you in the drive-through.

Recognise what matters in your life – your children, your health, your future goals – and focus your energy towards that.

Surround yourself with five people that have similar values, morals and ethics as you.

We are the culmination of the five people we spend the most time with. Choose wisely.

Trust your circle in life and business and ask for support. We can all have the greatest business intentions but if you don't have the time or support to amplify and empower your needs then it will unravel.

Great leaders ask for help.

Life coaches, accountants and bookkeepers, specialists, logistics, psychologists, friends, consultants, there are a lot of people that will make up your life and business pursuits and we all have a very real need to lean on someone sometimes.

Recognise that your team will also need to be well supported with encouragement and by providing opportunities because we can accomplish great things together.

Passion – fund your passion. Most of us have no clue what we want to do when we leave school, it isn't much better from eighteen to twenty-five, or after children, or study, or even after we are making money. Truth is, this is a struggle most adults will go through, but when you do find your passion, it's a game changer and it may not necessarily a full-blown career, it may be arts or creation or working a part-time role to support your mental health or balance your family life. If you want to be a lawyer but can't handle an eighty-hour week then law won't be your thing. Like sales, but can't handle rejection, then I have bad news for you.

What shit-sandwich do you want to eat, because ultimately, to gain what we desire, we will all be served one eventually.

It is understanding sacrifice.

Everything includes some sort of cost.

There is no free lunch.

It's scales. Nothing will be pleasurable all the time, but if it outweighs those terribly rotten days then it's worth a great shot.

'When you want to succeed as badly as you want to breathe, then you will be successful.' – Eric Thomas

Which leads me to the ultimate punchline, we are all here for an undetermined amount of time.

Some things matter, some don't.

Some things are important, some aren't.

But it's the things that matter and are important to you – your ethics and values that compliment your moral compass – are what drives you to succeed, and what gives you purpose.

For me, living a life with purpose doesn't mean you don't have life's baggage, past emotional trauma or stress, nor does it mean you need to contemplate the cosmic significance of your life while sitting on the couch eating a bag of chips.

It means getting off your ass and discovering what is important to you.

Don't look back.

Live in the present.

Be kind, be grateful.

Give.

And most importantly remember that when you live your life with purpose ensure you are true to your core values.

'Whatever you are, be a good one.' – Abraham Lincoln

CHELSEA MUNRO

Chelsea Munro is the award-winning creator and founder of Black Horse Naturals, a range of veterinary recommended natural products that assist in the health and wellbeing of horses and dogs.

Chelsea lives in south-west Victoria with soulmate and love of her life, Steve, along with her cheeky tractor-loving son and the extended family of many horses, eight naughty but adorable lambs and two small loyal terriers called Batman and Dixie.

She very much looks forward to the weekend visits of her adult daughter, Grace, where the family home becomes abuzz with love, life and laughter.

As well as writing, you will often find Chelsea enjoying all things nature, running, horseriding and bushwalking, getting sand in her toes, dancing to her very eclectic playlists, snuggling her family and forever finding the beauty in her everyday.

Chelsea is a champion of choosing happiness and is best known for her straight-talking, go-get-it attitude.

Having faced some difficult circumstances in her life, Chelsea continues to choose happiness and focus on breaking down the barriers that block those pathways to a happier and healthier life.

PAYING IT FORWARD

Danielle Loader

In this chapter we will discuss the concept of 'paying it forward' in business.

To pay it forward is an expression for when the recipient of an act of kindness does something kind for someone else, rather than simply accepting or repaying the original good deed.

***

Taking the leap of faith after twenty years in the industry, I utilise my skills and experiences and run the business with a big ethos of paying it forward where possible.

The recruitment industry, like many others, is about people and connections, and in my career, I have developed an extensive network and work continuously to nurture and grow this.

Maybe you are like me, you have years of experience and are an expert in your field, or you may be early in your career but have an entrepreneurial passion and drive.

'Life begins at the end of your comfort zone.' With courage and

confidence, belief in yourself and by paying it forward along the way, you can have a business that is successful, rewarding and fulfilling.

Here are five business tips of mine to help you and your business along the way, with an emphasis of paying it forward where you can:

1. IDENTIFY YOUR *WHY* — BOTH BUSINESS AND PERSONAL

When starting a business, it is important to identify and determine your *why*. When you know your *why*, your *what* has more impact and you will determine your business purpose. A business with purpose is one that attracts people more naturally.

Everyone's *why* is different and personal.

To take the leap of faith, I asked myself and determined my *why* from a business perspective but also on a personal level.

Ask yourself:
- What is the reason you want to start this?
- What is your service offering?
- What will make you unique?
- What vision/goals do you have for the business and yourself?
- Who are you doing this for?
- Who do you want to be? What managers and leaders inspire/have inspired you throughout your career?
- Who do you not want to be? Learn from toxic people and environments you have worked in.

My why is that I want to provide an expert recruitment service utilising, maximising and continuously developing my relationships, network and connections. To be hands-on and live my passion of helping people, 'changing lives' through placing them in new opportunities, training, mentoring or paying it forward.
I want to have a team that's inspiring, passionate and loves what they do, whilst giving them the flexibility to be with their families and offer balance.

I want to use our skills, talent and networks to help people where we can. All whilst embracing change where required, pushing my boundaries but still having a balance and positive mindset. I want to be present and maximise the time spent with my husband and children, whilst practicing gratitude and enjoying the simple things in life, with smiles and laughter.

This may seem a longer *why* than most business books, but by identifying your personal and business *why* you can look back to it when you need to – **you should never forget your *why*.**

2. IDENTIFY YOUR SUPERPOWER AND USE IT WISELY

We all have our own unique superpower. A person's superpower is their particular genius – the specific, unique and specialised skill that you bring to the workplace and also everyday life.

A superpower isn't necessarily a skill but a mindset, a way of working that enhances everything you are involved in. Some of us may not identify we have a superpower because it is something that comes naturally to us every day and is part of our make-up, so that we take it for granted, and in doing that, we do not maximise the full potential of it.

HOW TO IDENTIFY YOUR SUPERPOWER

- What do you love doing, what is your passion?
  - o At work and in business, there will be days that we jump out of bed with excitement for the day ahead. What makes you do this?
  - o Have a think about what sparks joy for you.
- What do you do best/what is your superior skill?
  - o Have a think about your key strengths. What comes effortlessly or what do you deliver on easily? Your superior skill will lie within something you are fearless about and ooze confidence in.

- o What skill do you take for granted that doesn't come naturally to others?
- Get advice – ask people who know you well what your superior skill/ superpower is.
  - o You may not see your superpower as easily as others do because it comes so naturally, you don't think it's a big deal. Ask people close to you and people you have worked/work with what they observe your superpower to be.
  - o Your superpower will be one that people around you can see clearly, and although you take it for granted, you have passion for it, do it well and with ease.

Your superpower could be anything, it might be listening to people, being empathetic, taking action, implementing and following process, it might be communication, coding, people skills, kindness – the great thing is it is unique to you, and as small as it may be to you, it is with no doubt big and great to others.

My superpower is my relationship management/people skills, and my passion is helping people.
I developed my customer service and relationship management skills from an early age, working in retail, customer service and hospitality where I would meet all different personalities. I really enjoy connecting with people and can easily speak to anyone at any level, connecting with entry-level staff as easily as an UHNWI who is looking for an EA to support them. This is something that I take for granted, when for others it could be quite daunting.
In the workplace I look to bring people together with my positive energy, mindset and drive.

WHAT TO DO WHEN YOU HAVE IDENTIFIED YOUR SUPERPOWER

Now that you have identified your superpower, maximise it and use it to help people and your business.

Be smart. Surround yourself with people that will compliment your superpower and each other's.

- Identifying each person's superpower will drive confidence and results. With them knowing they have a unique value to add to the team that no-one else has, this will drive motivation and a feeling of worth.
- Play to their strengths, rather than fight through all their weaknesses, delegate where possible to the person whose superpower it is.
- *'Another person's weakness is another person's superpower.'*
- Build a team, identify each person's superpower and create a small army of business superpowers – look at The Avengers!
- By also continuously developing and strengthening our superpower, we have the possibility of achieving extraordinary results and it allows us the greatest opportunity for success.

Paying it forward with your superpower is one of the easiest ways to pay it forward in business and life because this is a skill and unique ability that comes naturally to you.

Don't be afraid to '*be a unicorn in a field of horses*'.

As much as your superpower may be effortless to execute, it takes time and kindness to identify where you can use it for others.

With my superpower of relationship management and passion to help people, I set up free 'virtual coffee and learn' sessions, reaching out to guest speakers to collaborate and host, coaching and mentoring in an area of their expertise, connecting people.
I also founded a volunteer group, WR Angels, where I brought together very talented and like-minded women who wanted to pay it forward with their time and skills to help small charities or people less fortunate.

3. STAFF AND CULTURE

Your company culture is a shared set of values, beliefs and attitudes that guide your organisation.

A strong work culture boosts productivity, decreases turnover and improves employee engagement.

Sir Richard Branson has famously quoted, 'If you take care of your employees, they will take care of your business.'

A lot of companies offer great perks these days – free food, drinks, games rooms and amazing workspaces – but still, a human element can be missed and employees feel more like a number or a clone than an individual.

Happy employees genuinely care about you, the company and their work. Sometimes it's the human element that means more than the free stuff. Here are some ways to pay it forward to your staff that don't cost much but will go a long way and result in a positive, happy working environment and culture:

- Flexible working arrangements. With technology ever evolving, it is proven that anyone can do their job anywhere in the world, but some managers are still resistant to embrace this or feel supervision is required.

- With people's circumstances and timetables so different, even whether they are a lark or a night owl, we are all not our most productive in the set hours of 9am to 5pm.

  With the right tools and clear expectations in place on deadlines and performance, flexible working arrangements can result in long-term happier staff and maximum output.

- Show respect and empathy. Respect doesn't cost anything but can go a long way. In my twenty years of recruitment, one of the biggest reasons for people looking for a new position is because they feel undervalued in their position, not respected and not appreciated. To demonstrate respect, lead by example, genuinely care for others, actively listen to what others have to say before giving your viewpoint, praise openly and often, show empathy and check in regularly.

- Provide training and development and give responsibility. A top reason for people leaving jobs is for progression and opportunity. By investing in your staff and a good culture, this will increase productivity and performance, boost morale, aid promotion from within and boost a feeling of value in staff.

By paying it forward to staff using these tools, you will be creating a happier, more satisfied and motivated workforce. In return, long-term you will be able to attract like-minded talent that want to work for your business and join your happy, motivated team.

4. POWER OF CONNECTION

The power of connection is very important in business and in our personal lives. Connections in business are limitless and can allow you to benefit from the help of others, who you can offer support to in return and pay it forward to others along the way.

Any businessperson knows the importance of servicing existing relationships continuously and well. To maximise the power of connection also consider these three points:

- Continuously network with purpose and impact.
  - o The old-age business phrase of 'it's not what you know it's who you know' is still strong to this day. Building your connections should be something that is consistent and with purpose, plan who you want to connect with and why. Develop your LinkedIn connections daily – rather than just hitting connect, do it with purpose and impact. Send a nice message/personal note in the invite and then another to thank them for connecting and a short intro on you and your business.
- Ask for referrals/recommendations – give referrals/recommendations.

- o Good people know good people, 90% of our candidates we place in roles actually come from referrals and reaching out directly to our networks and connections. This is working smartly and strategically, providing a targeted approach for our clients. In turn you can pay it forward too by referring and helping people where you can. Giving recommendations of connections/people/ suppliers/products that you align with and have had an excellent service from can boost their business, and in turn, yours.
- Pay it forward, help others by volunteering.
  - o Earlier I discussed identifying your superpower and using it for the greater good. You can pay it forward with time and kindness, aligning yourself with a charity or volunteer group. Include employees by giving them a day off site to assist in a working charity bee, collection drive, clean-up or community help. This will empower employees with the gift of giving and help people or causes less advantaged along the way.

HAPPINESS AND WELLBEING

Wellbeing has been defined as the combination of feeling good and functioning well. We have discussed ways of paying it forward in business which have been focused around thinking of others, but in business it is also very important to think of yourself, especially your happiness and wellbeing.

Without considering and looking after *you*, your business could end up with a very short life span.

Points to consider for your happiness and wellbeing:

- **Work-life balance.** We have discussed the importance of this for your staff, so don't neglect yourself along the way. I have seen business owners burnout and lose their passion because they did not set themselves boundaries, couldn't handle stress and didn't take care of themselves by burning the candle at both ends. This resulted in them losing vision, focus, respect and nearly their business. Find your happy place and learn to reset and relax when needed. Practice the art of switching off (your phone too), especially with family and friends so you are in the moment and can enjoy the present.

- **Positive mindset.** Positive thinking helps with stress management; it is an art and can be mastered. Let go of the past and any negativity, learn from yours and others' failures and turn them into lessons. There will always be some people that don't want to see you succeed, don't listen to the noise. *'People will throw stones at you, don't throw them back, collect them and build an empire.'* The power of positivity is immense, and it can help you convert that energy into reality. We are all human and on days where we are struggling to be positive, reach out to a positive person in your life to uplift you. Positivity can be contagious – just as negativity can, so avoid negativity where possible and don't let people bring you down.

- **Practice gratitude.** Gratitude is thanks and appreciation that is heartfelt. You can practice gratitude in several ways in business and also in your personal life. You can support local businesses, leave a glowing review/testimonial, write a handwritten note of thanks, acknowledge and praise a work colleague, pay it forward, volunteer for unpleasant tasks, give a compliment or even just a smile. Gratitude is strongly associated with greater happiness; it can reduce stress, helps us sleep, relax our heart and heighten our happiness and optimism – practice daily without fail and reap the benefits!

There are many ways to pay if forward in business, resulting in a sense of fulfilment, not just success.

Once you have identified and determined your business and personal *why*, never forget it along the way.

By identifying your own superpower and your team members', you can continuously develop and strengthen them. We have the possibility of achieving extraordinary results and success maximising and building on our full potential and lifting each other along the way.

Look after your team and you will be surrounded by positive, motivated people who live your values and want to be on your journey with you.

Don't forget yourself along the way, running a business can be hard. Avoid burnout, practice the art of switching off and resetting and practice gratitude daily.

Ultimately, the person paying it forward grows as much as the person receiving the act of kindness.

DANIELLE LOADER

Danielle is originally from a small fishing village, Emsworth, in the south-east of England.

Relocating to London to study at the University of Westminster, Danielle graduated with a BSc in Business Information Technology. Working for a year at a national newspaper in recruitment advertising sales, a friend then recommended her for a trainee recruitment consultant position which was the start of her agency recruitment and consulting career. Here she utilised and built on her people skills and started her motto of 'changing lives' through placing candidates in new job opportunities.

She relocated to Sydney when she was thirty-three years old in 2011, after being head hunted to join a leading Australian recruitment company. Danielle now has over twenty years' experience in agency recruitment with most of her experience working for international market leaders and large national firms, winning numerous awards including Consultant of the Year, Cross Seller of the Year and Best Newcomer.

Now a mum of two boys, Oliver and Harrison, the agency recruitment industry was renowned for long hours, minimum flexibility, burnout and being cutthroat at times. Danielle wanted to change the approach, and as a working mum, have the flexibility to still do the job she loved, without compromising service, her home life and mental health.

Taking a leap of faith in January 2020 to utilise her twenty years of expertise and focus on building the now-international brand We Recruit. Group. She set up the We Recruit. Executive Support division from scratch, with focus in the global pandemic around building and nurturing relationships and paying it forward where she could.

Throughout this period she provided support groups to candidates looking for work and introduced free 'virtual coffee and learn' coaching sessions where she has collaborated with national guest speakers to coach and mentor, and continued with this post-pandemic, attracting large audiences and global speakers.

Danielle also set up a group of volunteers through the pandemic, WR Angels – where she brought together a very talented group of like-minded women whose focus was to help the community and pay it forward, volunteering their time and skills to help small charities and people in need. This has continued to grow and remains a future focus for Danielle and We Recruit. Group.

Launching into the UK market with the We Recruit. Group brand in 2021, their continued recruitment approach of not advertising on local job boards and instead nurturing and maximising their extensive networks by providing a search-based, tailored and targeted service for clients is unique and successful.

Danielle was an AusMumpreneur finalist for the emerging entrepreneur award in 2021, and as an organisation, We Recruit. Group pride themselves on being innovative and forward thinking, utilising new technologies and initiatives.

Still living her motto 'changing lives' and being very hands-on with recruitment, clients and candidates, Danielle's passion for people and helping them shines through in all she does.

LinkedIn: danielleloader
Website: werecruitgroup.com.au

YOUR PRODUCT IS PARAMOUNT

Emma Cook

I still marvel at the machines that we now use to cut our soaps. It wasn't that long ago that it was just me, cutting every single soap that we produced by hand. Today, we have two manufacturing facilities in Melbourne and I know that the machines will only get bigger as we keep growing.

To scale a product-based business when you are also the manufacturer is hard and it's definitely a long-term game. I can't describe it any other way than it being a really hard slog, but if you get the foundations right, then the possibilities are endless.

BACK YOURSELF BUT ALWAYS HAVE A PLAN B

'It's good to see a woman in these types of meetings.'

I still remember my reaction when I was told this by a much more senior colleague when I worked as a speechwriter for a government department. I was speechless and it ripped from my hands any confidence I had been able to gather when confronted with a room of much more senior men to brief them on what information I needed for a speech I was writing.

It wasn't the first time I'd felt this way – I had always felt confident in my work as a speech writer and previously as a journalist. But when confronted by a culture where you had to match it with much louder voices to get your ideas heard in meetings, job promotions, etc., I was struggling.

I needed a plan B.

My husband was originally the more entrepreneurial. It was the North American in him. He heard my constant frustrations and told me that we should start a business together. We came up with lots of different ideas for our business. In the background he was an emergency doctor who was constantly washing his hands. The supermarket-bought soap that we were using in our bathroom was the last straw for his dry and irritated skin. So, we started making soap in our kitchen.

Initially I balanced my new passion with my day job. I wasn't ready to give up the security of my fortnightly pay cheque. But it was when my employer denied me converting to part-time so I could spend more time on my fledgling business that I knew I needed to make some difficult decisions. I left my stable job with a clear deadline in my mind. If things weren't working after six months, then I had the confidence in myself that I would be able to get another job in marketing and communications.

That was eight years ago.

GET YOUR PRODUCT OUT THERE AS SOON AS IT'S PHYSICALLY POSSIBLE

So, there I was – at a local artists' market with my handmade soaps – waking up early every Saturday and Sunday, battling the elements, to sell my wares. A lot of people around me couldn't understand why I gave up a six-figure salary for something that appeared so wishy-washy.

But selling at the markets was never the endgame. It was the cheapest and easiest way to get my product in front of customers and learn very early on what it was that made them part with their cash.

Reid Hoffman, co-founder of LinkedIn, said famously, 'If you are not embarrassed by the first version of your product, you've launched too late.'

This quote has always resonated with me. I hadn't even finalised my ingredients or packaging and I cringe when I think about some of the concoctions that we came up with in those early days. White wine soap, anyone? But the way that people were reacting to the scents of the beautiful essential oils that we were using and the rustic look of our soaps, I knew that I was at least on the right track.

Yes, there were a lot of products that didn't have a life after my original market stall but there were also a lot of products that have gone on to become our most popular soaps. And that was because I spent a lot of time talking to customers about what they liked about our soaps and what sort of ingredients they wanted us to use.

I also learnt what was going to work for our product before we heavily invested in our manufacturing and our marketing. At one point I actually thought white wine soap was going to sell. What if I had poured all our money into manufacturing and marketing to launch the best version of our white wine soap possible to only discover that our customers didn't share the same enthusiasm in showering in alcohol? I wouldn't have just been embarrassed, I would have lost our business.

PRODUCT IS PARAMOUNT

I can certainly understand the argument that a good marketer can sell anything. But most of us, when we start a business, certainly don't have the large pockets that our established competitors have.

Very early on, I had explored the option of using a contract manufacturer for getting our soaps made as we grew bigger. I was unsure whether I had the technical expertise, or the confidence, to be able to move the way we made our soaps in the kitchen to our own manufacturing facility. It also meant that in those early years, I was stretching myself very thin being the person that also sold and marketed the soaps.

Taking on a contract manufacturer would have been the worst decision for our business. What has become our biggest strength is our own unique way of making soap. We may not have the marketing budget but we have products that we have spent many years perfecting and refining, using premium Australian ingredients. And that's what I'd like to think sets us apart.

As the orders have gotten bigger, it's been quite a journey in upscaling our manufacturing capabilities while continuing to make our soaps in the same way as when we were making them in the kitchen. But this has also been one of the most rewarding parts of my business journey and I still love being around the production of our soaps, taking in the beautiful aromas.

ALWAYS REMEMBER WHY YOU WENT INTO BUSINESS

When we first had the idea to make our own soaps, the journalist in me did hours of research. I learnt so much about the ingredients in most cosmetics and it was eye-opening. I had been told very early on by another soap maker that it was impossible to make a soap without palm oil. But the more I learnt about palm oil, the more I became resolute that we would never use it in any of our products.

The production of palm oil has been absolutely devastating on the jungles of Indonesia and Malaysia. And having done a lot of research on palm oil, I truly believe that the reason that it is used in so many products on our supermarket shelves is because it's cheap.

I also remember the light-bulb moment when I realised a typical liquid soap or cleaning product is mostly water in a plastic bottle.

Only this year did I put pen to paper and draft our company's vision, purpose and values. Despite this being something I probably should have done years ago, it was something that didn't take long for me to do at all. While they may not have been written down, it was these strong principles of wanting our products to do good in the world that has been able to guide many decisions in my business. It's also helped build trust with our customers, which is an added bonus.

In much the same way, I had to remind myself why I got into business in the first place when I became a mother four years into my business journey. While forging my own path was important, I also wanted to run my own business because I wanted to become more flexible and travel with my husband as much as possible who did a lot of remote work. I had always wanted to be a mother and it wasn't an easy journey for me. But when I had my daughter, my business was in an important growth phase.

For better or worse, I made the choice to be the full-time carer of my daughter for the first two years of her life. I was only going to have that time once with her and I wanted to make the most of it. My business was going to just have to work around it. I had a few employees working for us at that stage but I was still the CEO.

In hindsight, structuring my life around caring for my daughter was the best thing for me as a CEO, and I don't think it was a bad thing for the business, either. I had to put trust in the people around me and I also had to live more in the moment. During this period, I made the most of any hour I was able to give to my business and it's something that's stayed with me now that I am back working almost full-time.

WHEN IT'S TIME TO PIVOT, GO WITH YOUR GUT BUT ALSO THE NUMBERS

When you bootstrap your business and do everything in that business in the beginning, you run the risk of never being able to see the wood from the trees. I learnt this the hard way. At the beginning you are busy because you are doing everything. In my case, I was making the soap, selling the soap, doing the administration, the finances, etc. Obviously, I had to do this because I simply didn't have the money to have it any other way.

We were lucky in many ways that we were able to grow organically – most of our biggest stockists had pretty much hunted us out. Things were looking very healthy for us in early 2020. We'd just signed a couple of important international distributor deals and we were on track to double our sales in that financial year. There was no compelling reason to change the formula too much just yet. We were a small team of people who between us got things done. I was still wearing many hats – I was rarely pulled onto the production floor by then but theoretically I was working as our CEO, CFO, sales manager and marketing manager.

Then COVID-19 hit.

I will never forget the day we had tens of thousands of dollars' worth of international orders cancelled just hours before they were meant to be sent to port. I thought it was the end of my business.

The ensuing twelve months of business almost broke me. Not only had our international distribution deals been put on ice, retailers all over Australia were either forced to close or were not as willing to take risks with new brands.

I was starting to run out of ideas.

As painful as the last year and half has been for our business, it forced me to start really understanding the numbers and financial side of my business. I started my business to make soap and to create financial independence. Like most founders, I didn't start it spending hours poring over spreadsheets. And because business had grown quickly pre-pandemic, I really didn't have to. My biggest focus was trying to scale production and keep customers happy.

During an already stressful time, it was a difficult task, and something that I wasn't familiar with, to start really analysing my financial reporting and understanding the story that my numbers were telling me. But I'm so glad I didn't shy away from doing this. The numbers told me what we should be focusing on and where we needed to cut the fat. It's meant that despite a small drop in revenue, we've come out of a very difficult period more profitable than ever with a strong trajectory for growth.

SO, WHAT ARE MY TIPS FOR ANY BUDDING ENTREPRENEUR?

- Forge your own path but always have a plan B. Yes, to go into business on your own you have to take a leap of faith and back yourself but you also need to go into it realistically. The sad reality is that most businesses fail. Make sure you have a back-up plan if things don't work out.

- Get your product in front of paying customers as soon as it's humanly possible. It's tempting to fall into the trap of thinking that your product isn't good enough yet. But let your customers tell you what you can do to improve your product rather than just guessing.

- Your product is what sets you apart and it can do the talking when you don't have the marketing dollars to spend.

- No matter how far down the track you are, never forget why you started your business and never compromise on the values you held when you started your business. This will help guide you in your business journey and it will also help build a strong relationship with your customers.

- When it's time to pivot, trust your gut but always trust the numbers as well.

EMMA COOK

I am an award-winning journalist and speech-writer who had this crazy idea to give it all in in 2013 to start making and selling soap. I went from writing speeches for the Australian foreign minister to selling my sudsy creations at a local artists' market. And I wouldn't have it any other way.

Today, The Australian Natural Soap Company is stocked in over five hundred stores across Australia, including major retailers and online eco stores.

We have successfully upscaled our very humble production facilities (i.e. my kitchen!) to two manufacturing facilities in Dandenong, where we produce our solid and liquid soaps – still using the same unique slow-set process and quality Australian ingredients.

Along the way our products have won several awards, including a Nexty for our solid dog shampoo at the world's biggest natural products tradeshow in the United States as well as an Organic Beauty Award for our lemon myrtle face and body wash. In 2021, I also won the Mumpreneur Award for best sustainable product (Victoria/Tasmania).

Most of the Australian Natural Soap Company's products have come out of my family's own personal journey to reduce household waste so it's wonderful that our soaps have become an important part of other people's households.

All our soaps are also certified palm oil free. The palm oil industry has been terribly devastating for orangutans in Malaysia and Indonesia. We think one of the best ways to help bring about change is to offer real alternatives to palm oil products and to support organisations that are making a difference on the ground.

To date the Australian Natural Soap Company has saved more than

1.3 million plastic bottles from going to landfill and raised more than $40,000 for the Orangutan Project.

Website: theaustraliannaturalsoapcompany.com.au

CONFIDENCE REIMAGINED

Fleur Chambers

It surprises me how often, as an adult, I find myself thinking about our family dinner table growing up. I can still picture clearly the tapered legs that were a magnet for our small bare feet (if I had a dollar for each time I stubbed my toe!). I remember the splashes of paint and old pieces of sticky tape forever adhered to the sides of the table – a reminder of birthday presents wrapped lovingly years before.

Every night, Mum would ask one of us three children to tidy and set the table. This job would include rearranging all the random pieces of paper, books and bits and pieces into a consolidated pile down one end of the table. We all knew when my brother had undertaken this family chore because the pile was always on a precarious angle and the knives and forks were on the wrong sides. He blamed it on being a left hander, but I'm a 'lefty' too and somehow managed to do it right.

I remember the family dynamics, as reliable as those solid table legs. Every night at dinner my older sister would capture the family's attention by sharing stories from her day. She had a natural ability for accents and irony. My brother found his unique place as the only boy, safely nestled between two girls. Most nights I sat in silence. I listened. I observed. I'm not sure exactly when my quietness and my gentle ability to pay attention to my surroundings earned me the label of shy.

As with so many childhood traits, the lines between label and identity became blurred like chalk drawings on the pavement. Over the years, I settled without question into the belief that I was shy. I wrapped myself up in this identity like a warm and familiar blanket. I allowed it to protect me throughout my teenage years and well into my twenties.

After those family dinners where I sat in silence, I would hide away in my bedroom writing poetry and song lyrics. Growing up in the 1980s, I loved recording these poems and songs onto my pink cassette player.

I can still remember how heavy the red record button felt underneath my small finger. In these moments, I was held by delight and fear in equal measure. A rush of pleasure washed over me as I tapped into an internal spring of self-expression and creativity. This was met by a rumbling anxiety that my older brother may find these tapes and hold them for ransom.

Fast forward thirty-five years and here I am, forty-something years old, still gently observing and writing from the heart, still giving voice to my inner world and sharing my reflections on life into a microphone on my own.

I've moved from my two-tone pink bedroom into a professional recording studio. I've also moved from feeling fearful of being heard to deeply okay with being visible in this way, knowing that people in over forty countries are listening to my words.

So, what's changed besides a natural sense of maturity that washes over us all as surely as the tide washes over the sand?

It's simple. I've changed my definition of confidence. I've allowed this quality to feel more like a whisper than a roar. I've let go of my outdated beliefs – that confidence includes capturing people's attention, always having an opinion or grabbing every opportunity without fear or doubt.

I've embraced a new version of confidence – one that includes accepting myself, remembering my innate goodness, feeling valued by others and supported by life.

In this radical act of reimagining confidence, I've cultivated a level of freedom and self-belief that's enabled me to grow a thriving business as a meditation teacher, app creator, writer and philanthropist. In short, I'm succeeding on my own terms and it feels good.

This chapter is for you – the gentle observers, the deep thinkers and the meaning seekers. It's for those people who want to make a positive contribution to the world in a way that feels natural and in line with who they are. May the following ideas act as breadcrumbs along your path towards greater confidence, fulfilment and purpose.

IN ORDER TO GROW, WE NEED TO LET GO

Many of us imagine that confidence will arrive like an express post parcel when we add more to who we are. We tell ourselves we'll feel more confident when we gain that next qualification, have more experience or finally receive that praise or recognition from others.

Whilst there's nothing wrong with wanting to improve and add to your skill set or experience level, the problem with these *I'll be confident when …* stories is that they're based on a belief that right here, right now, you're not enough. When our actions come from an inner belief that we are lacking, they never offer us the satisfaction we desire. It's like pouring sand into a bucket with a hole in the bottom. It never fills.

Perhaps you can think back to a time when you received the praise or validation you'd been longing for and to your surprise, it didn't offer you the self-assurance you thought it would. Maybe you finally completed that course and instead of feeling confident and ready to go, you still felt like an imposter or unqualified.

These situations occur because the underlying belief that we are not enough or worthy still exists under the surface. We respond by looking for more metaphorical sand to fill our confidence bucket, we change our *I'll be confident when* ... stories and the cycle of chasing confidence continues.

So how do you break this unhealthy cycle so you can finally feel self-assured? The first step is to become aware of your *I'll be confident when* ... stories. With awareness you'll create space. Space to see these thoughts and beliefs with greater perspective and compassion. From here, you'll be more able to let these stories go. When you do, you'll feel less burdened and more free.

You can begin this process by grabbing a pen and paper and writing the heading *I'll be confident when* ... across the top of the page. Set your phone timer for five minutes and write down every story you tell yourself – even the ones that feel ridiculous (when my legs are longer or my nose is smaller!). Keep going for the entire five minutes. Read over the list. See it as separate to you. Take a few deep breaths. As you exhale, imagine that all these thoughts are leaving your body through your breath. You may like to rip this paper up, burn it (safely) or file it away. You can repeat this practice anytime you notice these stories taking hold.

EMBRACE YOUR HUMANNESS

We all know people who, in our minds, we perceive as naturally confident. We notice these people lighting up a room, capturing people's attention with engaging stories, ideas and plans for their future. Professionally, we see these people speaking up and promoting themselves in real life and on social media. In our minds, these people are always putting themselves out there without hesitation or self-doubt. We imagine that these people are never weighed down by the fear of not being good enough or being judged. In truth, these people are human just like you. They also have moments of self-doubt, fears of not being worthy and times when they feel like an imposter.

Inner confidence isn't about the absence of these qualities, nor is it about avoiding them. *Real* confidence involves accepting these 'shadow' aspects of ourselves and learning from them. It includes allowing these more human parts of us to be our teachers. Our insecurities, inner criticism and fears can, in their own unique way, help us to see what really matters in both our personal and professional lives.

Next time you notice the imposter syndrome creeping in or the voice of your inner critic getting loud – don't go to war with it. Try as best you can not to push it away (I know this is hard). Instead, pause and take a few deep breaths. Get curious. Notice where these thoughts and feelings sit in your body. Do they land as a heaviness across your eyes, a tightness in your chest or an ache in your belly? Keep breathing. Stay present. Ask these thoughts or emotions – *What are you here to teach me? What would you like me to know?*

Perhaps they'll urge you to stop comparing yourself to others, to rest or offer yourself compassion. Maybe they'll remind you to be brave or to forgive. Or will they gently whisper that you've lost your way and it's time to reconnect to your own wisdom?

BALANCE OUT YOUR NEGATIVITY BIAS

An important aspect of both personal and professional growth is understanding and balancing out our built-in negativity bias. As humans, we are wired to notice potential threats and negative experiences over opportunities and positive experiences. Whilst this negativity bias helped our ancestors spot the sabre-tooth lion prowling in the distance, these days our stress response often gets triggered unnecessarily. This can result in heightened experiences of fear, insecurity or concerns about being judged.

It's simple. If you want to create, grow or maintain a successful business, you need to spend time each day balancing out this built-in negativity bias. The good news is this doesn't need to take hours or cost lots of money. You can begin with just five minutes each day. Here are my two favourite practices for shifting from insecurity and self-doubt to trust and self-belief.

EXERCISE – SHIFT YOUR AWARENESS

Begin by taking three deep breaths. Recall one time recently when you did something that felt wholesome or positive (this act doesn't need to be extraordinary). Perhaps you were patient with your child or you really listened to a friend. Maybe you smiled at a stranger or wrote someone a thank-you email. Trust whatever example comes to mind.

Take a few minutes to explore this memory in more detail. Really picture who was there. Notice any emotions or feelings that were present. Offer this memory a smile. Allow it to remind you that you are a good person. Relax your body. Trust that this simple exercise has reorientated your awareness and strengthened your neural pathways for inner confidence.

EXERCISE – PEOPLE APPRECIATE YOU

Begin by taking three deep breaths. Bring to mind someone in your life who values you. This could be a family member, friend, colleague or client. Take a few minutes to call to mind all the different ways this person appreciates you.

This might feel hard so here are some ideas to get you going. Does this person value your good intentions, the way you desire to help others, to do the right thing? Do they value your good character, that you are honest, loyal or reliable? Do they value what's in your heart, your sense of compassion, care, joy or gratitude? Perhaps over the years this person has admired your skills, either innate or learnt? Or do they value the choices you have made in life, the way you have bounced back from adversity or taken risks? Maybe this person appreciates you because you offer them unconditional love?

Stay with this practice for at least five minutes, even if it feels uncomfortable. Really stretch yourself to notice all the ways you are valued. Allow yourself to really *feel* this experience.

This exercise is powerful as it acts like a mirror. Knowing you are valued allows you to value yourself. Doing this practice a few times each week will help you focus on your strengths rather than your perceived weaknesses. From here you'll make better decisions and move forward with courage and conviction.

YOU ARE SUPPORTED

It's so easy to think that confident people are self-sufficient and rarely ask for help or receive support. Part of redefining confidence includes feeling comfortable with receiving support from family, friends, team members and even nature. Far from being a sign of weakness, when we learn to receive support, we make bolder decisions, are less afraid to fail and more able to trust in the process.

Whilst I often take the time to notice how my family and friends help me, my favourite way to feel supported is to connect with nature – in particular, to learn from the seasons. Each season has a unique purpose, energy and lesson to teach us. We can use the seasons to help us make wise and skilful decisions.

Autumn teaches us to let go. In your business, this might include letting go of processes, projects, clients or even old beliefs that no longer serve you. Just as leaves don't resist as they fall from the tree, we too can learn to let go in our business without regret, resistance, stories of failure or disappointment.

Winter offers us the gift of reflection and rest. Just as animals hibernate in winter, there will be times when you turn inwards. During these times you may be reflecting on your achievements, exploring your own personal development or even enjoying some well-deserved rest.

Spring offers us the energy of beginnings, growth and transformation. During this season you may feel inspired to start something new, to expand or be more visible. Spring teaches us that we are safe to transform and reinvent ourselves and our business.

Summer offers us the opportunity to feel vital and alive. In your business this might look like rebranding, a new website, product or service. Or perhaps you'll experience a burst of energy and confidence to really promote your business or seek out new collaborations.

Make time to check in with nature and the seasons. Take a walk outside. Notice the colours. Become aware of the features of the season. Take a few deep breaths. Let nature offer you support and guidance.

BE INTENTIONAL

No doubt you've heard the expression 'where attention goes energy flows'. Starting each morning with a few intentions can help steer your day in a positive direction. Try reading these aloud each morning or create your own:

I trust that my insecurities, doubts and fears can be great teachers.
I take time each day to remember that I am valued and appreciated.
I know that I am supported.
I am confident in my own unique way.

Confidence doesn't magically arrive when we receive praise from someone we admire, earn a certain amount or reach a milestone in our business. We grow confident from the inside out by taking the time each day to learn from our fears, remember that we are appreciated and trust that we are supported by family, friends, colleagues and nature. Confidence is a practice. May you commit to it each day.

FLEUR CHAMBERS

Fleur Chambers is a multi-award-winning, internationally recognised meditation teacher and creator of The Happy Habit app. Her offerings have been downloaded two million times in over forty countries. Proceeds from all Fleur's projects go towards grassroots projects that tackle poverty in some of the world's poorest communities. Fleur believes that we can improve our own lives and contribute to the world in positive ways – one meditation at a time.

Fleur lives near the beach in Melbourne, with her husband, three boys and dog, Lucky.

REINVENTION & TRANSFORMATION
Jenny Pither

HAVING THE COURAGE TO TAKE A LEAP INTO BUSINESS

Anyone who tells you starting a business and working for yourself is easy, is either telling a good story, or very, *very* lucky. It's such an amazing learning curve when you first start out, and there are always ups and downs. There are moments when you really doubt your choices, but being open to continually learning from others and growing your business will see you working through challenges that can give you amazing benefits and rewards. Yes, it takes courage to start a business but sometimes, as happened with me, it can just be a nudge in the right direction for everything to fall into place.

Five years ago I was working in an administration role with an occupational therapist and her colleague. I had three young children, the youngest being five years old, and I was struggling to find a way to balance my work with being there for my kids. I really wanted some independence so I could be present with my children, and being an 'employee' left me feeling unsatisfied at work. I knew I had valuable skills. I'd been working in the medical and health industry for over twenty years at the time and with the experience of working with up to seventeen doctors in one practice, I had to be very organised and run a tight ship! It was also the early days of the NDIS and I was one of a small number of people who really understood the administration and software associated with it. The OT I was working with and her colleague acknowledged my very niche skill set and encouraged me to share those skills with other allied health professionals. The seed of an idea was planted and it didn't take long to convince me that I might be ready to take the leap of faith and work for myself.

SELF-BELIEF IF CRUCIAL TO REALISING YOUR DREAMS

I started Allied Health Admin Services in 2016 with an achievable goal in mind; to work for my clients for up to thirty hours per week. I had no doubt that I had the experience and ability required to assist health professionals with their admin and I also knew I had the specialised skills they needed. I believed working for myself would give me the flexibility to work around my kids, and if I achieved my goal, I would have the independence I desired. However, it didn't take long before word got out and I soon had double the amount of clients I had envisaged and had to take on employees of my own!

Five years on, and I now have seven employees and over twenty-five clients. I found that having faith in myself and my abilities, as well as knowing my niche, gave me the opportunity to grow organically. I knew what I was doing was helping and serving others in the allied health industry, so when it came to selling myself, it just happened naturally.

It was a tough decision to go into business for myself, but with the support of family, friends and colleagues I was prepared to take a chance, and I haven't looked back. It would be naive to think that owning and running a business is always roses. In fact, when you decide to go into business for yourself, be prepared for an incredible amount of learning and mistakes. When the going gets tough, ensure you don't lose sight of the big picture and what you set out to achieve. Ultimately, you're in business for flexibility and balance, right? So always continue to practice self-love, be kind to yourself and make sure that you run the business – it doesn't run you!

KNOW YOUR NICHE AND YOUR STRENGTHS

Since I branched out into the world of virtual assistants five years ago, the concept has evolved quickly. With the events of the last two years in particular, virtual and remote suppliers and contractors have become the most sought-after services, not just in administration but across a huge variety of industries.

When considering any career, whether that be as an employee or starting out on your own, you really must consider your strengths first, and then where your specialised skills – your niche – can be of service. For me, I developed my skills in a variety of positions in the medical sector. Over a long period of time, now over twenty-eight years in the medical industry, I have worked in radiology, general practice, occupational therapy, and with a variety of allied health providers. I began as a transcriptionist and receptionist, working my way up to lead receptionist before becoming an administrator coordinating up to seventeen doctors.

When I started my business, it was important for me to stick to my strengths and my skillset. It was helpful to link with like-minded people, other VAs and administrators in my industry, and networking with the professionals I was targeting. With my administration skills, I could have easily branched out into other industries and I have had interest from non-medical businesses, but then I would not be sticking to my niche; the area of work where I know, without a doubt, I can provide the highest level of service.

I've also found that my knowledge around the NDIS (national disability insurance scheme) has given my business an enormous boost. By being open and genuinely able to provide advice and support to my target market in this area, I was able to showcase myself without the need to advertise.

To this day, I have not needed to advertise my business to attract clients. I do, of course, have a marketing strategy around social media and my website, but we continue to attract an average of five qualified and engaged leads per week without the need for any paid advertising. That means those businesses are looking for us! Whether it's through word or mouth from our already happy clients and colleagues, or the positive comments we receive through Facebook and other social media, our business continues to grow organically because we fill a niche and provide a service that is needed within our industry. This alone is a true measure of where we stand in the sector.

Our clients always come to us with one common 'bruise' – ADMIN-ISTRATION. They are great at what they are trained to do, what they studied at university, but the day-to-day administration of a business may not be what they trained for and can be a pain in their side! This is where we excel and can bring a level of freedom to our clients and their teams.

By playing to our strengths, we have created a valuable service that is an asset to our clients, their ROI and even their stress levels! Whenever I'm networking and see women and mums introducing themselves and looking for advice about leaving their nine to five job, my simple answer is always the same; 'Know your niche, know your ideal client.'

SUCCESS DOESN'T COME WITHOUT FAILURE

We all start out in business with big dreams, innovative ideas and good intentions. We recognise a gap in the market, or we see others doing well in business, and believe we can do the same (or better!). Of course, no-one ever goes into business thinking, *I don't know if this is the right move, what if I fail?* If that were true, why would we even start? We must have some self-belief and a knowing that we can provide a high-level service or product that will be valuable to our community.

Having said that though, it's important to understand that with every new venture, I can say with 100% certainty that mistakes will be made. No matter what, mistakes are going to happen, and at times, you may feel like a failure. It stands to reason that when a roadblock or unexpected event occurs, and you are feeling as if you've failed, you can be left questioning your choices, wondering why you are even in business at all. But … you are starting on a new venture, you are facing complex decisions, often with little experience of running a business, and it's impossible to be in control *all of the time*! When you've had time to reflect, you will embrace these mistakes as a way to learn, grow and improve.

I've had many occasions over the last five years when I've been left feeling deflated, beaten and questioning my worth as a leader and even as a person! These roadblocks have come in many forms, but usually boil down to three main issues:

1. **Staff.** Managing staff is one of the most difficult factors in running a successful business and is not realistically anticipated when you first start out. Firstly, there are the general in-house politics and dynamics associated with different personalities in the team. Team members who don't get on, or are going through personal issues, can cause big waves in the day-to-day operation of the business. I've also had situations where my employees have let clients down or not completed urgent work, which has even resulted in a client terminating services. Managing emotions can also be difficult when valued staff resign, or when an employee needs to be dismissed for various reasons.

2. **Clients.** It took some time for me to work with clients around their expectations of what is achievable within their contracted hours and whether there is a capacity for overtime. Sometimes clients are not prepared to give and take. At the core, every client employs us to improve their business administration and processes – that's what they engage us for. However, clients are not always open or engaging with the changes we suggest.

3. **Family** – this is a big one! Ultimately, I started my business to have the flexibility to be present with my children and have some independence, but I'm often faced with the questions:
   - 'Is it really best for me to work from home?'
   - 'How does my work affect my home environment?'
   - 'How does my workload affect my children since my youngest is still in primary school?'
   - There are times I even find my business has an impact on my interactions with my husband, which can send me on an emotional roller-coaster!

Being my own boss, and working from home, I find it difficult to switch off and I know I'm not alone with this. Can you honestly say it's easy to walk away from your desk for the weekend? I'm always fearful of waking up to an email from an unhappy client wanting to terminate, or a team member letting me know they want to resign.

I've learnt over the years that failure is not a negative thing for us as human beings. How many times does a toddler fall down when they are first learning to walk? If they looked at falling down as failing, we'd all be crawling around instead of standing tall on our feet. We need to fail in some way to see the success of our efforts. This is not just about business, but every aspect of our lives. When we are learning to do something new, we could all say we failed in some way, but we learnt from each failure and 'got back on the bike' every time. Failure is not the reason you should give up, it's the reason you should *get* up and keep failing until you've mastered your skills. I see failure as a moment to GROW. Setbacks and failures are moments to embrace and learn from. I ask myself, *What went wrong and how can I do better next time to avoid this?* In order to be the business leader and mentor I want to become, I need these moments to help me to help others.

This is something I have learned through my business mentor,

Christina Joy. Her support and experience have continued to assist me to grow, learn and improve in my business processes, as well as my relationships. If there's one piece of advice I'd give anyone starting out, it's to hang out with like-minded people, and if you can, find a mentor who can guide you with their knowledge and experience, and keep you accountable. Prior to working with my mentor, I struggled to take on feedback of any kind. It wasn't just criticism I found difficult to deal with, but praise too! I know now that we must learn to accept all kinds of feedback, positive and negative, whether we like it or not.

I still have plenty to learn, and there isn't always an easy solution when you hit a roadblock in business, or in life, but I will continue to learn, and I certainly feel I'm on the right path to growing and improving as a leader and a person.

REACHING MILESTONES AND ACHIEVEMENTS

Never in my wildest dreams did I imagine I could win, be a finalist or even be nominated for business awards because of the service I provide to my clients and team.

To be honest, I always thought accolades and awards were for people who had degrees and excelled in their academic education. I didn't go to university, and going straight into the workforce when I left year twelve, I didn't feel I would be worthy of being a winner, or even a finalist, of such an acknowledgement. How wrong I was!

In 2018, I was encouraged to submit an application into our local business awards in the category of 'Best Startup'. This was for businesses in their first twelve months of operation and I thought it would be an opportunity for my business to reach a wider audience. Imagine my elation when I received an email to say I was a finalist in the category. Me – a finalist in a business chamber award! I didn't win in 2018, but the experience of stepping out of my comfort zone to even enter such a competition was amazing. When I entered the awards the following year for the category of 'Professional Services', I wasn't just stepping out of my comfort zone – I was leaping out of it! I knew some of the businesses I was up against, and again, a feeling of 'imposter syndrome' began creeping up on me, but hey – what did I have to lose? Whatever the outcome, I would have a great learning experience and get to network and be recognised by some of the most influential business leaders in our area.

Well, 2019 proved to be my year, and I was announced the winner of the category at the awards dinner! The experience and the recognition I received at my local business chamber awards in both 2018 and 2019 were proven to be my first 'real' achievements in business and supported me in every aspect of business growth. In 2020 I was nominated as one of the top one hundred small businesses in our area, and it was humbling to acknowledge that I was changing peoples' lives.

It was a pivotal moment for me when, in 2021, I was nominated and became a finalist in the 2021 AusMumpreneur Awards. Unfortunately, due to the COVID-19 pandemic, the organisers couldn't hold the awards dinner and presentation in person, but the event went ahead online and I was amazed at the achievements of so many inspiring women. Something clicked in me! It can be very confronting to acknowledge and 'own' our achievements, but it's these moments that need to be captured and acted upon.

The year 2022 has also proven a great start to my self-worth and business success with myself being named Outstanding Business Leader and the business as Highly Commended in the category of Excellence in Professional Services.

I have leveraged my achievements in the last few years to build my position in the sector. I have used what our team has created, along with my knowledge, to partner with a leading practice management software provider. A couple of years ago, partnering with such a prestigious business would have triggered my 'worthiness' button (!) but working with this company has been essential to our exponential growth. It has provided us with so many opportunities and I'm excited to see what's next for Allied Health Admin Services.

My advice for any entrepreneur starting out in business is to never limit yourself. Always be open to possibilities and NEVER think you might not be good enough or worthy of success. Put yourself out there! Eat the frog, go for the big deal; if it doesn't work, you've lost nothing … if it does work out, then who knows where it can take you.

PERSONAL GROWTH — MIND, BODY AND SOUL.

What first springs to mind when you read the words *personal growth*? When I first started my business and began networking with business owners, advisors and mentors, I had no idea of what was ahead for me in terms of what I could learn about myself and for my business.

It's fair to say my journey into personal growth and development has only just begun. 2021 was a big year with many milestones for me. With the events of the previous eighteen months, I was given an opportunity to assess where I was both personally and professionally. What is it I really want to achieve? And what do I need to do to make it happen?

I sought out professional support in the form of a business coach and I'm so glad I did! I'd recommend it to everyone, but a mentor/coach doesn't have to be in the form of a paid professional, especially if funds are short. You can share your thoughts, dreams and ideas with colleagues, or network with people who are well into their business journey and have been where you are. Keep an open mind about the advice they give, especially if you know they are experienced. You don't have to take their advice, of course, sometimes just talking things out can put things straight in your own head.

With the help of my coach, I've now been focusing on every aspect of my life; as a business owner, a boss, a colleague, a wife and a mum. I find that morning routines (or 'rituals', if you want to call it that) have helped me to look at life from a whole new perspective. I am grateful for every day and no two days are the same. I love to get to the gym four to five times a week after I've dropped the kids at school, and this sets me up for a positive and productive workday. At some point in every day, it's important to do something for yourself, something you enjoy, to settle your mind and give you some balance.

For you that might be through exercise, walks along the beach, coffee with friends or catching up with family. Several of my friends have taken up the challenge to take a dip in the ocean every day for the next 365 days! Whatever your vice, make it happen, as this will enhance your life in every way. Practice self-love and kindness without inhibition or worry over guilty pleasures – you deserve it – and no, you don't *always* have to be doing something for somebody else!

Now is the time to live an unapologetic life!

TAKE A LEAP OF FAITH

So, in summing up, does it take courage to venture out and start your own business? Hell, yes! But if you know deep in your gut that's what you want, be brave and go for it.

We're all on different journeys, so branching out on your own may not be for you, but my advice is when you feel opportunity knock, take some time to sit back and think about what it is you really want. What is your big *why*? Imagine where that opportunity might take you. Imagine how it would feel if you could wake up every day doing what you loved. Then imagine how you might feel if you were still in the same place in five years and hadn't taken the time to grow and develop. All growth requires taking a step out of the comfort zone, so if you feel a bit like a lobster waiting to break from its shell, analyse your strengths and your niche and see where it takes you. And then … never look back!

JENNY PITHER

Founder, juggler, wife and mum of three children.

Jenny Pither is all of these things. She is the face and name behind Allied Health Admin Services.

Jenny's passion for business lies in the allied health sector with a niche for the NDIS.

Jenny is known for her first-class administrative support for allied health professionals and as such has now taken her passion for what she loves and is known for to the next level. Jenny was a finalist in two categories of the AusMumpreneur awards for 2021 in the VA Institute category and Rural or Remote Business of the Year and named winner for Professional Services in the MidCoast Business Chamber awards in 2019. Jenny has also appeared in the podcast series with Cathy Love of *Private Practice Made Perfect.*

Jenny and her team don't work for their clients, but rather, work alongside their clients to ensure that at every step of the way they feel that they can focus on their core business and that is providing therapeutic supports to their clients with the knowledge that their business is taken care of and in safe hands. There is nothing better than riding on a high after positive feedback from a client that you have changed their lives and those of their family's by simply doing what you do best.

Jenny wants to empower and nurture other women and mums in business to believe in themselves. If they have a passion, a business or side hustle that they have dreamt will one day be a reality, there is no time like the present to pursue those dreams, start working on the logistics and building those business plans and goals so they can leave their nine to five jobs with confidence, to spend more time with their families and less time making money for someone else. Building a business from the ground up doesn't happen overnight but with small steps.

As a finalist in the AusMumpreneur Awards in 2021, and a collaborator in the AusMum business book, Jenny is hoping to use her experiences in business to guide, nurture and empower others to be themselves and to trust that they are capable to succeed in business.

INTO THE UNKNOWN

Jody Lee Euler

For many people, stepping into a new and unfamiliar landscape can be a terrifying concept and one they would avoid at all costs.

It's an interesting concept when you think about it, because we enter this world not knowing a thing. As a baby and then a young child, everything we do is a first and we don't give it a second thought. However, as life shapes us, often we lose that freedom of thinking and become more set in our ways.

Exploring new experiences and meeting new people has always been the source of my energy and for the most part of my life, I thought this was how most people lived.

After completing high school, I was fortunate to land a job as a photojournalist with our local daily newspaper, *The Daily Mercury*, and despite my inexperience, I was on a mission to deliver. It was a year that provided so much spontaneity and learning but it was the year that followed, attending Design College Australia, that really shaped me into the creative I knew I was born to be.

After three years working as a freelance graphic designer in Brisbane, learning from the good, the bad and the ugly encounters, I returned home to a job in the advertising department at the Mackay *Daily Mercury*.

While the work really didn't challenge my creative desires, the ability to work to tight deadlines was a huge opportunity to learn and a skill that would stand by me in the years ahead.

In 1997 I threw caution to the wind and launched my childhood dream. The world of redhotblue was born in my mum and dad's rumpus room, and the heart of the business then was graphic design and advertising. I knew it was time to find my own office space when Mum, on a regular basis, was manoeuvring my paperwork off her ironing board and Dad was strategically sidestepping my artwork layouts as if he was on a boot camp obstacle course just to get to the other side of the room.

When I think back to this time, there's a distinct link to that concept of learning as a child. I had no fear, but instead, the thrill of the chase spurred me on. I remember thinking, *What have I got to lose?* I took a 'no regrets' approach to all I tackled. I thought to myself, *This may not work, but at least I'll never wonder what if?*

Six years later, 2003 turned out to be a significant year that catapulted my brain to a new stratosphere.

I was recognised through the Australian Institute of Management Awards as Young Manager of the Year for our region. In 2016 I went on to win Owner Manager of the Year. Redhotblue was also one of five finalists at the Telstra State Small Business Awards. With my team, my husband, parents and sister we celebrated in style at the Gala Awards held at the Hilton in Brisbane.

While being acknowledged among so many outstanding businesses was a memorable and proud moment, meeting one of the judges proved a pivotal turning point. The judge who would become my business mentor for three years was the true gold of the night.

I always say he took me under his wing, but his version was that I latched on and didn't let go. Either way it was a chapter in my business career that changed my thinking and ultimately allowed the growth of redhotblue.

One aspect of business I didn't realise at the time was as my business grew there was a necessity to have systems and procedures in place. No longer was my skull a place that I could store this information. Instead, a mature business approach was needed. The other part to growth that I didn't count on was the management of people.

Over the past twenty-five years I've had the privilege of working with over fifty team members and the majority have been incredible individuals, some of whom are still my very good friends today. However, there was a lesson ahead that I was about to learn.

Every individual had different values, experiences and personality traits. Maintaining the redhotblue brand promise I had worked so hard on elevating was hinging on how to ensure I kept my team aligned and advocates of redhotblue.

What I know for sure:
- Being true to yourself is one of the most important ingredients for success.
- A business strategy and marketing plan is crucial, but never underestimate gut instinct.
- The road ahead is long, enjoy what you are doing each and every day.
- Always take a moment to reflect on how far you have come.
- Appreciate your staff, your clients, your suppliers. 'Thank you,' and respect costs nothing, but means everything.
- The value of an unexpected thank you is priceless.
- Business is hard, days are long and tough decisions will test your strength, but the journey should always be something you love. The day you stop enjoying it is the day to say goodbye and move on.
- Wearing many hats does not prove you are an excellent multi tasker, it diminishes your focus. Learn the art of delegation.

Sitting in a comfort zone has never been my style, and in 2012, redhotblue expanded to offer event management services.

Nothing we did was small and in a very short time frame we had become known for our large-scale extravagant events. Transformation of football fields and airline hangers into black tie galas. On numerous occasions we transformed Mackay's quiet city centre into a hive of activity with street activations that attracted crowds of more than thirty thousand people.

However, the event that will forever hold a special place in my heart was a charity event created with my dear friend and past employee, who was diagnosed with terminal ovarian cancer. This wonderful woman was determined to make a difference in the time she had left. In 2016, The Nude Lunch was born, and the name was a perfect representation of all she was going through. Stripped bare, leaving her feeling vunerable and emotionally and physically exposed.

Little did we know how successful we would be and how far her message would reach. During the five years of delivering the event, it grew from a 450 seated event in an established venue to 845 guests housed in an extravagant big top marquee in a park by the ocean. With the COVID-19 virus pausing many live events, in 2020, we delivered The Nude Lunch virtually to a national audience of five thousand.

I enlisted local businesses to help me build a temporary broadcasting studio from where the event was live streamed. The three-hour live digital event attracted celebrities and well-known entertainment personalities from across the nation.

After five incredible years, during which time more than $400 thousand was donated, my co-director and I decided it was time to lay this event to rest. It was a gut-wrenching decision but as one door closes, another one opens.

On hearing the news, Ovarian Cancer Research Foundation approached my co-director and me to become Queensland Ambassadors.

It was a true honour and one that saw us deliver the national fundraising event, Frocktober, into the Mackay community for the first time. The 2021 Mackay event broke a fundraising record from a single such event for Ovarian Cancer Research Foundation.

What I know for sure:
- Always believe in your ideas but have the evidence to back them up.
- Understand that sometimes you must lead the way, even if you are alone. With conviction, others will join you.
- Recognise opportunity but also recognise when change needs to occur, regardless of how tough the decision may be.

Of course, business hasn't always been awards, limousines, colourful moments and celebrations. There have been some very lonely roads, dark days and times where I have considered, *Maybe this is the end.* The mining downturn affected businesses across the globe, with the Mackay region also taking a direct hit. As I watched long-standing, prominent businesses close, I knew the tide was also rising around me. The large companies we had worked so hard to secure stopped spending money on all marketing activities, and as the domino affect reached us, it was a time of great despair.

In 2015, I had all but made the decision it was time to close redhotblue, but the one thing that kept me from saying those words out loud was my incredible team. The culture of redhotblue and the wellbeing of my employees had always been my top priority and I was about to witness just how deep that ran.

Our creative director called a meeting and as I sat at the boardroom table listening to everyone volunteer a pay cut to ensure we stayed afloat, it gave me courage to keep going. I was overwhelmed by the compassion shown from my team.

We dug deep, stayed true to who we were as we watched so many other businesses in our industry sell their souls and compromise their service offering. Within a year we had bounced back.

What I know for sure:
- Mistakes are only mistakes if you don't learn from them.
- As a business owner, at times you'll need to make tough decisions, but before you do, seek advice from the right people to ensure you have all pieces of the puzzle.
- Don't compromise on your brand promise – adapt when you need to, but don't lose the core of why you started and who you are.
- Always act with integrity, even when others don't.

When I consider the title of this chapter, *Into the Unknown*, most of my experiences fit this heading perfectly, but none as spot on as what I was to learn in 2008. At this stage in life, my husband and I had two daughters. Tia, who was two and Piper, who was six weeks old, and I had been in business for eleven years. Like any new parents, we were completely unaware of the complexities these little beings could bring to our life. However, navigating the challenges presented by our firstborn was like learning a new language.

I vividly remember the phone call that kickstarted my journey into a foreign landscape. 'Hi Jody, it's Sarah from the Mackay ASD Clinic, we are phoning to make an appointment for your daughter Tia.'

After a momentary pause, I asked Sarah, 'I'm sorry, what is ASD?' Her reply floored me. Autism spectrum disorder. I managed to stumble my way through the remainder of the conversation. I hung up and burst into tears.

I remember thinking, *How could this be possible?* Tia was advanced in her learning and had progressed through milestones quickly, how could she have autism? Yes, give her the wrong-coloured plate and a complete meltdown would occur, but we just put that down to the terrible twos.

I knew there were quirky mannerisms we had witnessed in her few short years of life, but when I'd question this with doctors, they'd simply respond that she's just a free spirit with determination.

The journey we embarked on was one that would change our lives forever. Not just as parents, but as individuals.

There were two things that became apparent during the volume of local appointments. I needed to learn – and learn fast – and we needed to work with the experts who were only available to us in our capital city, Brisbane, either a ten-hour drive away or an hour and a half flight. Tia and I ended up flying to Brisbane fortnightly for the most part of the year.

Six months later, just before Tia's third birthday, she was diagnosed with Asperger's – which is part of the autism spectrum disorder.

While eager to know all we could to help Tia, we were confronted with three facts that remain seared in my mind:

1. There is no cure.
2. Early intervention is key if we want to give our daughter the best chance in life.
3. A substantial number of marriages with a child on the spectrum don't make it.

The third one for me didn't even register. I thought to myself, *Surely we just need to be the percentage who do,* but it was the second fact that set my compass in an entirely new direction.

Attending workshops across the state and reading as much as I could became my new obsession. The regular flights to Brisbane where Tia would attend small group classes while I sought support from parents was a turning point.

The hardest aspect of Asperger's is that most people see these individuals as 'normal'. It's a term I hate, as who truly is normal and what defines it?

For my daughter, and many with Asperger's, they wear a mask daily. It's the best stage show production you will ever find. Lights, camera, action – however, the backstage pass is where the true person can be found and often where the pieces fall apart.

Meltdowns would occur over the smallest of things, preventing us from leaving the house on time on a daily basis. Ironically, the *unknown* for people on the spectrum is their biggest fear, so a very different approach had to be introduced to our lives.

In the early years, I made every conceivable aid I could. We had visual charts on walls to ensure there was some level of certainty for each day. I wrote a book every year that sat in the classroom for the teachers, parents and other students to shed light on a topic that many had never heard of before, let alone understood.

As part of my quest to bring about awareness and support to a regional city, I decided to put my business skills to use. In 2013 and 2014 my team and I delivered sell-out workshops to more than five hundred parents and industry professionals with a world-renowned expert on Asperger's.

I have lost count of how many medical and specialist appointments we have attended over the past decade. Navigating unchartered waters is a place of loneliness and desperation and a journey that no-one can prepare you for.

It's not only about supporting the individual with Asperger's, but the entire family that also needs to adjust. Our youngest daughter, Piper Rose, is the true warrior in this story. Not only for her physical strength (she's an aspiring young gymnast), but her emotional intelligence is beyond her years.

Many would say she knows no different, but as a mum there is a constant tug of war in my heart. The little voice in your head at the end of the day when exhaustion kicks in. Daily, I poured myself into every strategy for Tia, but did Piper get the love and attention she needed?

If I consider the life canvas that has been uniquely created by our family, I'm not sure any art critic would know what genre to place it in. Our approach to life has two distinct styles. One half is filled with a kaleidoscope of colour and the remainder a very defined and structured black-and-white pattern.

Some may call it abstract; others may think it's a mess, but it's our masterpiece and one that I'm proud to stand behind.

Sure, there are days where I wish it was a simple landscape, but our world has never been paint by numbers, nor would I want it to be.

I'm grateful for the lessons I've learnt through the daily challenges and constant juggling act. The ability to problem-solve quickly has become my normal and appreciating the small moments in life that many take for granted is a gift I may have never received.

I still remember the first kiss Tia placed on my cheek and the song that was playing. She was eight years old. Sensory issues prevented her from wanting to be touched for most of her childhood years so hugs and kisses were out of the question.

To not be able to embrace your daughter when she needed comfort or just to express, 'I love you,' was a steep learning curve. However, at the end of the day, a hug filled my cup but emptied Tia's, so who was the hug really for?

I still attribute that Piper was the reason Tia learnt to show affection. Observing behaviours is how people on the spectrum learn and what better teacher than a daily dose from your little sister who loves unconditionally.

It's not that people on the spectrum don't love or feel emotions, it's just they show it in a very different way. To accept and understand, this is the true meaning of love.

What I know for sure:
- Don't close your mind to different ways of thinking. A new perspective can provide answers you may not have considered previously.

- When everything seems impossible, take ten minutes to stop. Nothing good will come from decisions made in a heightened state of stress or anxiety.
- Your mind can either be a powerful ally or an enemy of destruction. Use it wisely.

I'm so grateful for those who have inspired me, encouraged me, believed in me, supported me and never given up on me. Family, friends, colleagues – without them I could not have travelled this journey. However, I also respect the opposite scenarios that have taken place. The challenging and confronting moments, the loss, heartache and grief, because these lessons too have shaped me in a manner that provides a full perspective on life and everything that is truly possible.

Be yourself, be brave, create without limitations and live a life of no regrets. Stepping into the unknown may just be the greatest decision you've ever made.

JODY LEE EULER

Jody Lee Euler is often described as someone with boundless amounts of energy and a creative mind that is forever turning visions into reality. From a young age Jody had a thirst for creativity and leadership and was often initiating a different way of thinking amongst her peers.

Today, this is evident from the many business success stories she has delivered during her thirty-year career. Her longest standing business and greatest passion of twenty-five years is redhotblue – a creative marketing agency located on the Whitsunday coast in regional Queensland, Mackay. The company, who comprises of ten specialists, deliver work throughout the region and across the nation and have been recognised for their work at a number of prestigious awards.

Jody has been recognised at the Australian Institute of Management Awards on two occasions in 2003 as Young Manager of the Year and then in 2012 as Owner Manager. In 2003, redhotblue was also recognised as one of five finalists in Queensland at the Telstra Small Business Awards. Over the past two decades the company has won countless awards at the Queensland Multi Media Awards for their exceptional design and advertising work.

In 2016 Jody, became a co-director of the charitable organisation the Nude Lunch (Ovarian Cancer Exposed) and was a driving force in establishing and growing the event. The organisation was born from her dear friend and past employee who had been diagnosed with the disease and wanted to make a difference in the time she had left.

In 2020, when most events across the globe were coming to a halt due to the challenges of COVID-19, Jody simply changed gears. She led her team at redhotblue and a committee of volunteers to deliver the event nationally via digital means attracting celebrities, sporting legends and TV personalities from across the nation. Jody played an integral role in the organisations success donating over $400 thousand in its five years of existence.

She was invited to become a Queensland ambassador for Ovarian Cancer Research Foundation. In 2021, along with her co-director of the Nude Lunch, she brought the national fundraising campaign, Frocktober, to Mackay for the first time to a sell-out audience of three hundred women raising $25 thousand on the night.

During her highly energetic career, Jody entered a partnership and formed Core Magazine launching a monthly lifestyle magazine distributed across the Mackay, Whitsunday and Bowen Basin region. The publication recently celebrated ten years in print.

Jody has volunteered her time throughout her working career having served on several boards including the Mackay Community Foundation. Throughout 2021, Jody dedicated her time to running a podcast, Homemade Heroes, with her co-host to shine a light on unsung heroes in the Mackay community.

Jody won gold in the 2021 AusMumperneur Awards taking out the regional business award for Queensland and the Northern Territory.

Despite the numerous achievements, at the top of Jody's list that she holds closest to her heart is motherhood. Jody is the mum of two teenage daughters (Tia, fifteen, and Piper, thirteen) and is incredibly proactive in the autism space with her eldest daughter being diagnosed with ASD at the age of three. She has brought internationally renowned expert Professor Tony Attwood to Mackay on two occasions to sell out audiences in her ongoing desire to better educate the professionals and parents in the region on how to support these individuals.

Her husband of twenty-one years along with their teenage daughters, Italian greyhound and Burmese cat, live walking distance to the beach and enjoy the lifestyle a region like Mackay has to offer.

Jody is someone who represents authenticity perfectly. She lives by one of her favourite Dr Suess quotes: 'Why fit in when you were born to stand out,' and is often seen dressed in her signature colour orange that matches her fiery red hair.

She has brought streets to life, created spaces for the youth to explore their creativity, opened the minds of conservative thinkers and spoken at numerous events often bringing about change.

Jody has delivered work across numerous industry sectors working with a diverse audience of professionals including: fashion designers, engineers, government representatives, the mining sector, developers, scientists, estate agents, young entrepreneurial startups to companies with a strong global presence.

Her ability to take clients on a visual journey and excite them with possibilities they may never have imagined is where she feels most at home.

Website: redhotblue.com.au

REINVENTION

Resilience, overcoming adversity
and thriving in business
Justine Martin

I am known as the Queen of Resilience. I have been to hell and back a few times, faced my mortality and built a couple of successful business along the way. With the pinnacle of obtaining gold, silver and bronze in the 2021 Ausmumpreneur awards and Gold in the Roar Success Awards.

In 2011 I was diagnosed with remitting relapsing multiple sclerosis (MS) and told I would never be able to work again – my world crashed and I questioned my purpose. Then I underwent three heart surgeries in 2013, 2014 and 2015 followed by pericarditis where my family were called in. In 2016 I developed a purple rash on my extremities known as livedo reticulosis, my kids thought it was great that I was turning into a zombie, this then led to being diagnosed with melanoma and ending that year with mixed cryoglobmenia. 2017 was a hell of a year with being diagnosed with chronic lymphocytic leukoma (CLL), small lymphocytic lymphoma (SLL) stage four and having to undergo chemotherapy with the fight of my life, all while planning for my future. I had to become pliable and persistent with what life was throwing at me, all while remaining positive.

My chapter is how I overcame these adversities yet continued to grow as a person, sharing with you my five tips to resilience that has led me to be a successful award-winning entrepreneur.

1. PURPOSE

I was diagnosed with MS when I was forty years old, a disease that my own mother had died from complications from when I was just twenty-six. I had to stop work in my dream job a month after being diagnosed due to my symptoms of fatigue, memory issues and that I could no longer count, use money or tell the time. A job and passion that I had worked up to in my career in the weight loss industry. I've always had a calling to help other people. I remember my neurologist telling me I would never be able to work again. The world became a very dark place for me for a long while. I questioned everything, what my purpose would now be in life, what was I going to be to society. I felt like a huge burden to everyone.

My income had stopped and I became solely reliant on another human being. My partner worked in the mines, so he earnt too much money for me to get any government handouts. Our expenses increased with all the medical tests; specialist bills, plus adding into it the cost of the medications I was on. I had gone from working full-time, bringing in a good income, to being stuck at home looking at four walls and having to ask for money to buy survival items such as food and clothing for myself and my daughter. I had always been able to earn my own money, now I had a medical professional tell me that was never going to happen again.

The one thing he did tell me was to find a hobby to fill my time. I chose art. I had always wanted to learn how to paint but had never found the time due to chasing my career. Now, all I had was time. I finally walked into the painting class, after three months of driving there, parking outside and having huge anxiety and then driving home in tears as I was too afraid to walk inside. Then one day I got really angry at myself, parked the car and went in and discovered a whole new world. I could create! I would lose myself in painting. It turned out I was very good. I sold my first painting for $300 five months after I started learning. I could still earn money and not only contribute by paying taxes again but I had found my purpose in making people happy through looking at my art.

As I went through my cancer journey, people who ask me how I was so resilient and positive. It then occurred to me that my story of coming through all the adversities I had faced was someone else's survival guide and that was giving them hope, again adding to my purpose.

To identify your own purpose doesn't have to be a hard thing to discover. Often, it's staring right at you. I love using mind maps for direction, using a mind map was really helpful in working this out, and when you work out your own purpose, life takes on a whole different meaning.

2. PLANNING

Some of the best-laid plans fail, often due to circumstances out of our control, and that's okay. I know only too well about planning for future events and goals only in the blink of an eye to have it all change. But you can always rebuild. Yes, it takes time but it can be done with planning, goals and persistence.

So why plan if things can and will change? Because I have found overall it boosts peak productivity, which leads to success.

My first point of call is to use a trusted system with everything at my fingertips. Whether you use electronic or paper is up to you. I personally use a paper-backed system with a planner. I have tried using electronic e.g. Trello boards. Yes, I always have my phone with me, but once I lost my online calendar due to a faulty update, and by switching to a paper system, everything is always there written in black and white. It also gave me an excuse to buy a gorgeous new bag to carry it in. I have cognitive damage due to the MS and short-term memory issues. I have to write everything down or I don't remember it. If I don't write it down it leads to poor planning, and poor planning leads to zero income, and no-one wants that, especially me!

Don't be a mater and try to remember everything, because you won't. People ask me all the time how I have achieved so much even when things have gone so wrong, and the first thing I say is I use a trusted system. I'd really be lost without it.

My planner is set up into sections. In the front I have contact details, followed by my daily calendar. I prefer a page to a day for hourly appointments with the opposite page having my A list and B list of things to do.

In the back half of the planner, I have it divided into various sections tailored to my needs for notes which dividers labelled meetings, journal, medical, book, JUZT art, Van-Go decals, Resilience Mindset, new ideas, kids, holidays, goals and lots more. As each section fills up, I transfer the notes to their own labelled folder in my office, making it easy to locate for reference at a later stage.

Within my trusted system it's important to have SMART goals. I use a mind map to set out what my goals are, keeping a copy of the map in the front of my planner. Streamlining my goals so that they are Specific, Measurable, Achievable, Realistic, Timely and they are 100% mine. Be sure to have daily goals, they go on your A List, things that need to be done that day. Everything else goes onto your B List. Update these every afternoon, so you know what you have to achieve the next day. Make sure you reward yourself when you achieve your goals. I no longer use food as a reward, but I may buy a special outfit, get a massage, my nails done, my hair done or go on a holiday, depending on the size of the goal.

Never let someone else's false beliefs stop you from achieving your own goals. If you believe you can achieve it, set your mind to it and do it.

3. PLIABLE

Never be afraid to give something new a try. If you have a new idea, go for it! What do you have to lose? What if you actually succeed with that idea?

Things are constantly changing in our environment. I have found that being flexible and not allowing myself to be stuck in a certain way, just because that's the way I've always done it before, isn't always the right way. I don't give up, I modify.

When I was going through my cancer journey, I lost the ability to use my hands properly. I couldn't hold a pen or even a paintbrush. Here I was with my new purpose having it ripped away from me. Painting is my happy place. It's the closest I get to meditation.

I was tagged on Facebook in a lot of videos of an artist overseas who finger-painted with oil paint. I wondered if I could achieve a similar effect with acrylic paint. I got some disposable gloves, and found that through the chemo nausea, I was able to still paint and create something magical just with my fingers. I developed a new style. One that I still use today and now teach to others through finger-painting for grown-ups classes. I could have sat there and cried, *Oh why me?* but I didn't – okay, maybe I did for a day or two, but then I got off my pity party and tried something different for the slim chance it might just work. And it did! A lot of what I create today still has an element of finger-painting in it. The freedom it takes my mind to is something I had never experienced before.

Being pliable is the key to resilience. It's all about how fast you can bounce back. It's okay to have a sad day. I still have sad days when my body or mind is failing me, but I make a conscious effort not to stay with that emotion for too long and do something that makes me happy.

4. POSITIVITY

I get asked a lot about how I can be so positive after everything that has happened to me. My answer is always the same. We make our own choices. I choose to be positive. It takes far less energy to be positive than to be negative. I surround myself with like-minded positive people. Build your own tribe. We are the sum of the five people we hang around with the most. If there are negative people with no future positive goals in your inner circle, move your friendship to an acquaintance, and start building that positive tribe, your positive inner circle. You will feel a difference in your output and general well-being.

Control the fuel going into your minds. I no longer watch the news; it very rarely has anything uplifting or positive on it. Why does it always have to show negative stories? The answer is simple: it doesn't, but the media choose the stories. I don't worry I'm going to miss hearing about an important event, as it will come up in conversations with friends. I can then do my own research on it. I unfollow people on my social media if their values don't align with mine, I'm still friends with them but I no longer see their posts in my newsfeed, and they don't even know.

I watch positive impacting TedX talks, listen to positive podcasts and read motivating biographies. Do something that will motivate you and put you in a positive mindset. I'm told often that I'm an inspiration, which is humbling, but I'd much rather be known as motivating people to change what they are not happy about in their own lives. Action rather than reaction. Helping them gain their own success.

I regularly visit a counsellor to offload my feelings. I don't want to over-burden my family and friends with what I go through with my body and mind on a daily basis. I feel it's not their responsibility. I'm always smiling. Why? Because to smile is infectious and is the easiest way to bring happiness to others.

5. PERSISTENCE

How is one persistent? You keep showing up no matter what the situation is. Every day, I get out of bed no matter how crap I'm feeling. I make my bed every single day, even on my worst days. Why? Because no matter what rest of the day holds, even if it means spending it on the lounge (mostly with my laptop), by making my bed I have achieved one thing that day! Nothing is nicer than walking into your room with the bed made and sliding into a nice made bed. Your quality of sleep is far better too.

I keep moving forward in life, I reflect on the past but I don't live in it. I have my SMART goals set and work on these each and every day. Yes, even on my days off. I am still filling in my daily planner and being persistent and consistent.

Never ever tell me I can't. I take that as a challenge. I am open to new ideas, some of my best ideas happen in a moment. I use Mel Robbins' theory every single day with the *5 Second Rule* to action every idea. How? I write them in my planner for future reference so I don't forget them, then I can action them again at a later stage.

If something isn't working in your life then change it. You always have the ability to change, no matter how hard it is to do so. Don't let fear of failure or fear of success stop you. I never sit and whinge, that takes too much energy that I just can't afford. Instead, I again do a mind map and look at all the options in changing what I am doing. Then persist with it and create success one step at a time.

Resilience means having the capacity to recover quickly from difficulties and to show toughness. I am a resilience consultant and I help clients work out their own purpose in life that gives them direction to succeed – it makes it a lot easier in planning their business to be profitable and successful. Keeping in mind that when adversities come your way, and they will, you need to be pliable in order to gain resilience. You can't be positive all of the time, but it sure makes a huge difference in yours and everyone else's lives around you if you are. And don't forget to smile.

JUSTINE MARTIN

Building resilience and overcoming adversity are two terms cemented in Justine Martin's world! Never did she image her personal journey through life would take this course, but from the debilitating challenges she was faced with, it would test her strength daily.

Eleven years ago, Justine was diagnosed with multiple sclerosis (MS), she underwent three heart surgeries and was then diagnosed with three primary cancers. Justine was told she would never work again. But that was never an option for her!

Justine catapulted herself into the world of business. She not only changed her life to give it purpose and direction, but also inspired those around her with her story.

After learning how to paint and using her art as therapy, Justine's talent was recognised across art shows and exhibitions. Most importantly, at the time, she felt like she had a purpose – her art was making people happy and that made her even happier! She started winning award after award. Justine is now greatly recognised in the art world by her peers, and is a multi-award-winning artist. This gave her the confidence and belief in herself, and she found the strength and determination to take control of her financial future.

She has since expanded JUZT art to include wellness classes, Zoom painting classes, commission art pieces, Van-Go Decals, finger-painting for grown-ups, team fingerprint (corporate team-building) and a new publishing house.

But it didn't stop with one business and JUZT art was just the beginning. Justine discovered that her challenging personal journey of how she built her resilience, changed her mindset and conquered her adversities became an inspiring story for others. Justine started public speaking at events, and became an ambassador for MS Australia, speaking publicly about her story. She was very comfortable speaking publicly, and soon discovered her story and the ability to connect with others really made a big difference.

Justine then launched Resilience Mindset, a consulting business to help others facing resilience and adversity issues. The success of Resilience Mindset lead her to expand her brand, launching the Resilience Top Tips Pack, an eight-week course, podcast series and working on her book to launch 2022.

Justine credits her unique business to her personal life experiences, 'My life experience has enabled me show true compassion and inspire those with their own health issues and life-limiting disabilities to build their own resilience and confidence through creativity at JUZT art, and compassion, direction and purpose through Resilience Mindset. The services are set up to give hope and a sanctuary for my clients to escape day-to-day hardships through the art therapy classes and the one-to-one personal resilience coaching.'

Justine's greatest inspiration and determination comes from her mum. At age forty her mum was diagnosed with cervical cancer, and then in 1997, when Justine's daughter was just seven weeks old, her mum died of complications from MS after being diagnosed with lung cancer. Her mum was forty-nine years old. 'There are so many similarities when I compare my life to hers and the one thing she has inspired me to do is never give up – thanks, Mum!' says Justine.

Her story and inspiration has been heard and acknowledged Australia-wide, she recently won five awards at the 2021 AusMumpreneur Awards including gold for Coach of the Year. Then Justine won gold at the 2021 ROAR Awards for Creative Artist of the Year. Her awards and accolades over the last decade have bolstered her resilience, self-belief and her position as an industry leader in resilience coaching.

Website: justinemartin.com.au/resilience-consulting
juztart.com.au
Linktree: linktr.ee/justinemartincorporation

WHEN WE RAISE EACH OTHER UP, THAT IS WHEN WE RISE

Karen McDermott

EMBRACING COURAGE

I have been in business for ten years now. I suppose you could call me an accidental entrepreneur as I did not set out to build a publishing empire. I actually went on a pursuit to help stories get told and it has brought me on an amazing journey, one that has required me to be both courageous and confident.

When I took the leap into business, it wasn't so much a decision. It was more of a calling. I wasn't one for putting myself out there, but my calling required me to take *me* out of the equation and put my mission first. And when I did that, I started to show up for story.

I had the audacity to just step into this role and own it and share it. But it wasn't fuelled by any ego. It was fuelled by a mission to help stories get told. Because stories connect. They heal, they ignite, they educate, they create memories between mums and kids and parents and guardians.

There are so many wonderful things that come out of story that I *couldn't not* show up and answer that call. It all started with me sharing my own story in my first novel. Not only was it therapeutic for the people who read it and connected with it, it was also the most therapeutic process I ever went through in my life.

I could feel myself getting healthier, my atoms were healing because I was releasing all this heaviness that I had held inside me. I had done this unconsciously, but I couldn't help but imagine the potential if I shared my journey so that others could do it with intent.

So, I answered the call and started to take steps into business, and I set an intention and a goal. I started with the law of attraction. I set an intention to build a million-dollar press, but I wasn't in any rush to do it. I was raising my children, but I was also showing up, and I was very focused.

I just allowed things to grow, and whatever I needed to learn or do would be revealed in the next step. The courage to take my leap into business came because I was called to it. I answered the call, and then there was a guiding light. I really connected with my power of knowing.

I had faith that it would navigate me on the journey that I endured. Because when you know how to know, you are fearless. The wonderful Katy Garner from The Women's Business school commented at the 2019 AusMumpreneur conference, 'Karen, you are fearless,' to which I replied, 'There is no fear in knowing.' I have since gone on to write a book called *The Power of Knowing* to help others make decisions with unwavering confidence.

At the beginning of my business journey, my strengths were not something I really considered because at the beginning I had to do it all. I didn't have the luxury of staying in my genius zone. But more than anything else, I was just showing up, being authentic and being myself and sharing so that others could benefit.

There was definitely a serving mentality behind my work. There always has been and there always will be. This is what lights me up. I love guiding people to realise their potential because so many people are still asleep to the possibilities of what they can achieve just by showing up.

I have been doing this since 2008 and I intend to keep doing it and just see where it goes. Never in my wildest dreams did I think that I would reach my goal of a million-dollar press within seven years and to have so much fun doing it! I thought it would take at least twenty-five! During the journey, I have discovered and unveiled different strengths in myself that I didn't know I had.

If I believe in something, I don't give up, so if I think about something, there's no way I'm not going to do it. I'm all about going on the journey and letting it happen and accommodating it. I'm a very hard worker when I'm passionate, and that's my superpower.

BEING COURAGEOUS THROUGH CHALLENGES

With success, there's always going to be challenges. Challenges are inevitable. Teachings and learnings are inevitable. When you go on any quest, no matter whether it's in business or in life, there's always going to be what you feel like are failures. But I believe you've never actually failed because you're always learning, you're always growing, you're always moving towards something bigger.

So, I have a different perspective on challenges, which is that they come when we need to learn something new that evolves us into the person we need to be. Who says failure has to be negative? Who says that challenges are bad?

They're there to shift your perspective. Whenever I see a challenge come, I get a bit excited and I go, *Okay, there's so much room to grow here.*

Failing, to me, is *not* pursuing it, not going on the journey, not listening to the signs and just compromising too much of yourself in pursuit of your goals. You never have to compromise yourself or your values in order to achieve success. Because when you do that, you never get to experience success as good as it can be because you have compromised too much, so that whenever you get there, it just doesn't feel worth it.

CONFIDENCE ON THE JOURNEY

We're forever growing. Success in business, for me, means going with the flow, manifesting, making it happen and staying out of dramas along the way. I just enjoy the process. I understand that things happen for reasons and sometimes these reasons are beyond our control.

I've always been very intuitive. I've always been connected to my power of knowing. I never lost the ability to *know*. I believe that a lot of people don't understand or don't realise that they too have the ability to know. Too many people are leaning outside for the answers, when we should be looking inside for the answers and outside for the support to make it happen.

I believe that's a very big thing that a lot of business owners need to understand, and when that clicks with them, things will flow so much better. Just allow things to happen. Set intentions, actions and inspired thoughts.

I understand myself. I prioritise joy. Too many people become business owners and stress. Yes, there's going to be times when things are heavy in business, but understand that is not going to be what it's like all the time.

Think about what does bring you joy and start doing more of that. And that is where my next call is taking me. I will always publish books and have authors. But my next call is to help authors and mothers realise that you do not need to sacrifice all of yourself. You can awaken to your potential, and we can show our next generation that anything is possible.

When your heart, mind and values align, you can make anything happen.

I work with some beautiful beliefs:
- There is no such thing as competition, only opportunity to collaborate.
- We are here to help each other along on the journey, even those who seem to be ahead of us.
- A loving perspective will always return the best result.

- When you prioritise joy, you will always be successful.
- There is no fear in knowing, when you learn how to know you can make decisions with unwavering confidence.
- Welcome feedback with open arms, but close the door on judgement.

WORKING WITH THE UNIVERSAL LAWS

I have studied the universal laws and there is the law of reciprocity. And that law means that what you give out, you will receive back. It may not be from where you expect to receive it. But when it comes back to you, you will feel it, you will know it.

And when you're grateful for it, then it keeps the cycle going. That flow, that toing and froing. And one of the things that some business owners don't realise is that reciprocity is one of the fundamental parts of being a business owner. You're probably doing it and maybe not even realising, but when you are aware of it, you can use it and be mindful and grateful for it. And if you have a giving heart, then you're going to be abundant in many ways.

Since becoming an entrepreneur back in 2012, I want to help people. A powerful motivator for me is to help people. But one thing I had to realise was that I couldn't block the receiving aspect. Otherwise, the flow and the cycle of growth and evolution can't be at its highest potential.

Yes, I had growth, but I couldn't reach my highest potential because I was very blocked off to the receiving, and I thought that the financial gain was the receiving. But receiving is so much more than the financial exchange. So, when I attended the AusMumpreneur conference in 2015, my mind opened up to the power of the flow. They're rising each other up in the giving and receiving and that all felt so much more natural to me and it opened my mind to how wider and how bigger and how much more powerful that type of business mentality can be.

So, when we create the opportunities we want to experience, but open it up so that we can share those experience with others, well, that is what is super special. That is what makes the world go round and I wanted to be in that space. After the 2015 conference, I started to think bigger, about how I could serve others, but also serve myself in the doing and also just to keep it all full circle. One example is that I hired a castle in Ireland because I wanted to go on a writer's retreat and I thought, *Well, this is a dream for me so it might also be a dream for others.* In that doing, it was not only serving myself, but I was also serving others and we all benefited from it. I am a big advocate of the win-win scenario. The results were better than I ever imagined. The castle was an amazing setting. It really and truly did bring the whole experience to the next level.

In my receiving and in my giving, there was ebbing and flowing and natural progression for all involved. And when you understand the universal laws, of which some believe there to be eleven, reciprocity is really an integral part of it all. That is why I believe that we need to take a moment to understand and embrace it. Because when you understand it, allow it to be and you work with it, then you are going to reach your highest potential because it's going to keep serving. It's always going to be a universal law, so it makes sense to take the time to understand it, focus on the positive aspects and make it work for you. In doing so we grow beyond our wildest dreams.

When we work alongside them, we see that they enable us to have our best life. It's important to keep our soul motivated, ignited and alive, and by working with universal laws that will keep you motivated and driven.

Another thing to be mindful of is that every time there's a cycle in your life of evolution, of setting an intention, just remember it comes full circle. And when it comes full circle, that is a time to stop and pause. A lot of people do not realise the power in the pause. I just want to share a bit about that for a moment as I am currently writing a book on it.

Burnout happens, especially for business owners when we don't value the pause. The pause is just as productive as the charging forward and the actionable items that we do. It is so important that we embrace the power in the pause. Because when we pause, we fill our cup up. In the pause, we recalibrate and recharge so that when we get back into our minds and body, our soul is all aligned so that we're ready and we're in our best self for the next cycle so we can serve it better

An example of this is when I work with the rhythm of my kids going to school. When my kids are on holidays, I shift gears in my mind, I have a different rhythm. I use these times to write because author-mum is a nice mum. But most of all I hang out with my kids, even if it's just hanging out at home, we're present together and it serves me well.

My body and my mind have got into the rhythm of every nine or ten weeks we have a two-week break, every year we have a six-week break. It does take courage to adapt but you will be surprised at how people respect it. Over the past few years, I've conditioned people into understanding that February, when the kids start a new school year, is also the annual starting point for me.

I'm currently in my sixth year of doing this and I'm consistently recalibrating and decluttering because every one of my nine-week cycles, what served me in the cycle beforehand will not be serving me now. In doing this, I make room for the magic of the next cycle because too many of us are carrying around things that we need to declutter as those opportunities and things that no longer serve us will be of great value to someone coming behind.

THE POWER OF *NO*

For a yes-person, learning to say no is not only important, is it courageous. I was always a yes-person, but as I grew much bigger in influence, there was no way that I could be the present mum that I want to be and say yes to ALL of the opportunities that were coming my way. I struggled with this for a time, so much so there would be nothing left for me or anybody else if I just kept saying yes.

I have come to know exactly what opportunities are in line with my current intentions because I'm very connected with my power of knowing. And when I know it's a yes, it's a definite yes and I have the courage to action it straight away. But when it's a no or I don't know, I have the courage to say no. *I'm sorry, that doesn't work for me right now.* You can still say no and be a loving person!

In the words of Derek Sivers, author of *Anything You Want*, 'It's either a HELL YES or it's a HELL NO!'

And that's one of the keys to success. It's a very big key thing in business and it's actually part of the art of reciprocity because when you learn to say no to things that your heart is not in, it means you're in the energy and aligned with the people on the energy who are a yes. When your heart is happy, then everything keeps moving and growing because everything grows through love.

What many of us don't realise is that we are constantly working with or against the laws of the universe, and when we take time to understand these laws, we can maximise our life potential because these laws do not waver for wealth or hierarchy – we are all the same, the difference is the energy we produce. From a business perspective, it pays to arm ourselves with knowledge about the ebbs and flows of the universal laws. They work equally as well for good as they do for bad so it is so very important that those of us who strive to make the world a better place through the work we do, take the time to understand the laws enough so that we can manipulate them for good to ripple out into the world. In doing so, we actually keep the energetic gates open for that goodness to come back to us, either in financial rewards, opportunities or whatever means we intend.

There are no limits to what we can achieve and by giving the best of ourselves with the right intention we will receive the best in return and YES, we can expect that to happen! Absolutely expect the universe to provide, there is enough for us all.

KAREN MCDERMOTT

Karen is an award-winning publisher, author, TEDx Speaker and advanced Law of Attraction practitioner.

Author of numerous books across many genres – fiction, motivational, children's and journals – she chooses to lead the way in her authorship generously sharing her philosophies through her writing.

Karen is also a sought-after speaker who shares her knowledge and wisdom on building publishing empires, establishing yourself as a successful author-publisher and book writing.

Having built a highly successful publishing business from scratch, signing major authors, writing over thirty books herself and establishing her own credible brand in the market, Karen has developed strategies and techniques based on tapping into the power of knowing to create your dreams.

Karen is a gifted teacher who inspires others to make magic happen in their lives through her seven life principles that have been integral in her success.

When time and circumstance align, magic happens.

Website: serenitypress.org
kmdbook.com
mmhpress.com

MANAGING ADVERSITY

Karen Perks

SECTION 1: FROM THEN TO NOW

THE EVENT

I had always believed, and practiced, the mantra of 'fail to plan, plan to fail'. This mantra provided structure in how I would succeed through life, a simple yet determined mindset to achieve financial and personal milestones and success. And in essence, had always been part of any successes to date.

What I hadn't factored into my mantra was a life-changing event. The one when the air is removed from your lungs, you can't breathe, and the ground opens to a deep, dark, bottomless and empty nothingness. The one when you realise you are not going to be who you thought you would become, and the one when you will never be the same again.

This was 2004. What started as a year of excitement with the birth of my third child due in August, finished as the beginning of the journey of the new me. During this year, six weeks after my youngest was born, I became extremely ill with a viral infection that went to my heart. I was diagnosed with cardiomyopathy – heart failure. Three children under seven, and my husband at the time, were also about to begin this journey with me. A journey of reinvention through adversity.

THE IMPACT

A single comment from my cardiologist after the diagnosis was, 'I recommend you don't look on the internet.' I am not sure if anything could be worse than being told you had fifty-fifty chance of living past two years and even less past five years. What could the internet tell me that would be more devastating than thinking of not seeing your children grow up?

The first few years are still a blur. Living from one specialist appointment to the next one. Assessments if my heart was making any recovery on the medication. Explaining to my children why I can't walk and talk at the same time, and running was a distant memory, although now I have a great excuse why I don't run.

The physical impacts were obvious, the emotional were silent. I eventually came to terms that my career was not going to be the same. What it would be, I could not even dare to dream, imagine the opportunities, start to plan out a new future. It was such a long way away.

Five years later, I mentally needed to have purpose and started back in the workforce, ever so gently. Starting with a part-time position and gradually moving into full-time management positions, the lessons of corporate expectations were constant. What I needed was flexibility, and what was not available was flexibility. I needed the flexibility to perform my duties – either at home or with flexible work hours – yet I was required to be in the office, work late or on weekends. I realised that I could never achieve management positions in corporate businesses with their current expectations. I had to find another way to fulfill my destiny, and not be limited in my belief of what I wanted to achieve.

WHY A BUSINESS?

Jump forward ten years to my first consulting business. The reason for starting became an easy decision when mass redundancies were made in my industry. Sometimes you just need the 'gentle' push, and it should have been the obvious path – formal full-time positions were not working for me physically, emotionally and spiritually. I needed to be in control of my own path.

This is not to say I don't work too many hours, weekends and early mornings. What I am saying is that I can manage my energy levels, I know when I need to prioritise workloads and I make decisions that are in my, my family and the business' best interests.

There is ample evidence of why people with a disability should start their own business. My own very real evidence agrees that traditional work environments do not meet the needs of anyone with a disability. I think I have become very cynical of the corporate brochures.

What I have discovered on the journey of being a business owner is how adversity is both a curse and a blessing. I have needed to become so self-aware that the Dalai Lama would be very proud.

The business decisions I make are influenced by my health experiences that changed my views on the world, and how I believe that business can make positive impacts to people, be inclusive and that they have a responsibility to do so. My business journey reflects what I discovered about me and how I integrate those beliefs and what I can share to make someone else's journey a bit easier.

SECTION 2: FINDING COURAGE FROM ADVERSITY

Courage is a word often used by business owners. I often question myself on where I find courage. How do I be innovative and brave in competitive areas? What is the difference between courage and recklessness? How can I use my lessons of courage in my business? It is lifting to feel that I can face any challenge with the belief that I can quieten the fear as it can't be worse than the past?

WHAT IS COURAGE?

According to Merriam-Webster, the definition of courage is: 'Mental or moral strength to venture, persevere and withstand danger, fear or difficulty.' By this very definition I should be the queen of courage after facing years of withstanding fear and the difficulty of not being able to live a life.

There are so many days when I haven't aligned the mental perseverance of scaling a business to being courageous. Being courageous to me is physical prowess and overcoming obstacles. However, it takes incredible courage to be in business. Making decisions about the future, new products, responsibility for team members, mental health of those around you your customers and financial responsibility, just to name a few. These all take courage. I remember being told that the worst thing you can do is not do anything. I understand why – because you are crippled by fear. Fear of the unknown, fear of the what-ifs if something goes wrong. My view is that you should fear doing *nothing* more than *something*.

HOW TO BE COURAGEOUS WITHOUT FEELING COURAGEOUS

During the years from 2004 until 2009, I didn't associate that I had courage. Yes – I was fighting every day. Being able to sit up in the hairdresser chair was a major accomplishment. It was during this time that my mantra – 'fail to plan, plan to fail' – would be my saving grace, and on reflection, supported me to be courageous. Planning is the key to reducing stress. To go shopping (there was no online delivery in 2004) was a logistical challenge and often faced with fear. Fear of collapsing, becoming so fatigued you looked like you had just finished the Boston marathon. Planning the outing gave me the courage to achieve a shopping outing, and a successful one at that.

It is the little steps that build your internal courage. That rebuilds your own internal belief system that you can move past the unknown, the what-ifs, and, *What happens if I fail?* Determining what failure meant to me gave me the courage to plan beyond it and have my own built-in net to catch me when I fell.

COURAGE IN BUSINESS

How can I use my lessons of courage in my business? Internal strength is not obvious, but more a set of built-in actions and behaviours that are triggered to overcome fear. For me, courage is to aim for the stars knowing I have built-in fail-safe nets. This could be setting new financial goals with a new product release and committing to expenses such as marketing or new positions. I maintain the courage to be focused on the result, i.e. meeting those targets with the comfort that the other product lines are profitable to cover the committed expenses.

Courage does not mean foolhardiness in business. That is pure recklessness and guaranteed short-term failure. Knowing you have contingency measures through planning ensures that I maintain my levels of courage to focus for the stars.

SECTION 3: EMBRACE THE EXPERIENCE FOR BETTER BUSINESS DECISIONS

From 2004 to 2009 I was never ready to dream about my future. Major life-changing events are just that. Life-changing. You cannot hide the fear in your eyes, the loss and the disappointment in yourself. Work is intrinsically embedded in our lives, and hierarchy in the workplace feeds self-esteem in traditional workplaces.

For me, there was incredible loss. I felt less – less as a person and less of what value I could add to society. From the age of sixteen, my career aspiration was to help businesses. How could I do that if I couldn't help myself?

In recent years I have been challenged to lead my business into social media campaigns where I was the lead. During 2020 and 2021 I took the opportunity to attend every training session I could and had a breakthrough in a one-day professional development course on social media campaigns. What I learnt that day is that what I perceived as my fear of failure was one of the most common fears in the group of women.

Social media makes you vulnerable and I was utterly challenged about being the face of the business and the responsibility that came with it. I had to find my courage to ensure that social media is an active part of our marketing strategy and not limited by my actions.

WHAT SKILLS AND EXPERIENCES MAKE YOU A BETTER BUSINESSPERSON?

I love reflecting – it allows you to see what went well and what you can do better next time. Continuous improvement is the technical term. If I had to list what soft skills I have learnt about the post-2004 me, and what values I represent, then I am very pleased with the now-me. I bring those values to the business. We give more than we take, we ensure we guide our clients with information knowing ethically they can make informed decisions for their business. We trust and fulfill on that trust.

I look internally to ensure we align to businesses with similar values and behaviours. We don't make any excuses for not being true to and respectful of our team.

SECTION 4: PERMISSION TO SUCCEED

Who do I need permission from? some would ask. Well, *myself* is the answer. Success, or the journey to success, can bring stress. And stress on my heart is not good. Defining success in business has taken reality checking to ensure there is a balance between meeting my goals and not impacting long-term health outcomes.

For me personally, there is an intrinsic link between my own self-efficacy and success. I have struggled with these connections for many years and continue to find the balance between defining success on a personal level and the business. This has impacted business decisions, speed to market and the size of the business.

As a business owner, it is important to not allow adverse experiences inhibit the business. It is critical to ensure that you know why you are behaving in certain ways and the impacts on others. An example is a key team member was reviewing the social media programs and making rec-ommendations. They were all very sound recommendations and ones I would suggest to any other business. So why was I resisting the changes? Because I hadn't given myself permission to succeed, and whilst the social media campaigns were not performing to their maximum ability, then I was safe where growth would max to. Until I identified why I was behav-ing in this way, then business growth was always going to stifle.

Being able-bodied for thirty-seven years brought many opportuni-ties and life experiences. There were very few times when I didn't do what I wanted. There are intrinsic emotions when loss occurs, and you change. Embarrassment is an interesting emotion, and I am not sure that I was embarrassed, but there were many times of *why me?* Running away or hibernating are more common emotions and behaviours. Being conscious of these emotions and appreciating the impact they have on you personally is the most important thing to ensure that you do not get in your own way of your business succeeding.

SECTION 5: TO SHARE OR NOT TO SHARE

In 2021 I began submitting the business into business award categories. There was one I deliberated over for weeks on whether to make an ap-plication. I felt we had a strong chance of being a finalist so it wasn't the credibility of the business I was concerned about, it was that the award would identify the business – actually me – as having a disability. I had always been proud of the fact that I could achieve equally – even if it was a struggle. The biggest challenge is that some corporate clients still judge my ability to meet deadlines. Everything we do in the business has strict deadlines – non-negotiable deadlines. Where do my needs of flexibility and managing workloads convert to 'putting in the extra yards'?

I submitted the application, became a finalist, and then won the award of Business Disability Excellence (NSW). Then the questions started – as no-one knew that I was carrying such disability, many asked what we had been doing for the disability sector.

The award was a personal achievement that is very special to me. It is an acknowledgement of being able to succeed under such adverse and difficult circumstances and shining through. It means I have moved mountains under adverse conditions. It means I can be true to the new me and not forget the wonderful qualities I bring from the old me. Maybe I can create a new mantra.

OVERVIEW OF TOP FIVE TIPS:

Managing adversity is a long-term commitment. The commitment to be true to your old self and your new self. The sense of loss is real, I know I am not the same person I was prior to 2004. Applying skills learnt through adversity to my business has helped to create a more meaningful and connected business that is empathetic to others and encompassing to all. My wisdom would be to:

1. Be courageous.
2. Embrace the new you.
3. Be true to yourself.
4. Be truthful with who you are.
5. Don't accept other people's limitations.

KAREN PERKS

My name is Karen Perks and I am the founder and managing director of Bid and Business Writers. I have a Bachelor of General Studies (Education) from the University of Queensland and currently studying my MBA.

We are a successful team of business consultants that specialise in business writing of tenders, grants, business plans, proposals, information memorandums and award writing. Located in Newcastle, New South Wales, with an office in the UK. Our team of consultants are specialists across all our services and are educationally qualified and industry experienced.

In our first year of trading, we were a finalist in four award categories and gold winner in one. A proud moment in our history. We were very proud of these results and appreciate the peer acknowledgement of our work.

My story is one of managing adversity and how that impacted me at initial diagnosis and ongoing both personally and professionally. The business is an important part of my life, it allows me to challenge myself professionally which typically is a self-reflection moment on my personal life.

I became extremely ill six weeks after my youngest child was born. What should have been a warning sign was not being able to lift a 6kg baby out of her cot, severe pain in my legs and stomach, couldn't walk more than 20m and couldn't depress a clutch in a manual car.

My condition deteriorated, and in less than two weeks, I was in hospital being visited by the chaplain and had the first of three pacemaker/defibrillator inserted. With doctors' comments of 'we are not sure' and 'you are too young' ringing in my memory and innocent comments from receptionists of 'you must be very sick as we are moving patients to fit you in'. Not the most comforting in the cardiologist rooms.

The reality is that this story may be about my journey, but the unspoken heroes are my family, both immediate and extended. My children had to bear the brunt of my limitations and although we did this journey with a smile, I am forever grateful for their resilience and love. Resilience developed out of necessity.

This single life-changing event has created a ripple effect of my own reinvention so many times. I have had to reflect and manage the adversity in both my personal and professional life.

My professional and personal lives are so intertwined as is often the case for those living and working with a disability.

I hope that I can inspire anybody who has or is experiencing life-changing events to see how they can use their experiences to leverage into business. Adversity is not limited to physical disability; it can be anything that impacts you to a level where you are forever changed. The takeaways are to be true to you and know that you are loved and supported by many.

Website: bidandbusinesswriters.com.au
Linkedin: ancientwisdomwriters

THE ART OF REINVENTION

Mafae Yunon-Belasco

One thing I learned in my earlier years of life is that change is inevitable. We are bound to go through change whether we like it or not, and this can be seen in pretty much every aspect of life. We don't always have control over when we change, but I have come to find that we do very much have power over *how* we change … and that is where reinvention comes into play.

Starting a business is like giving birth to a child. You don't always know what to expect, you don't know who to run to, and more often than not, major things happen when you least expect it. But one beautiful thing that I've held onto all these years in business is that courage, intentions and the faith that you have in yourself play key roles in your ability to carry on, reinvent and thrive with your business.

As much as you plan and strategise, your business will have a funny way of running its course. Sometimes it turns out different from what you initally intended. However, despite the many changes it undergoes, everything falls into place eventually.

Even when you're just in the ideation phase of your business, fear is present. In the decision-making, in the signing of important documents and in the obstacles that we face daily, fear is almost always there. Trust me, I am speaking from experience.

As I started out in my career, I partnered up with individuals who I thought were great people to execute my mission and vision. For a while, we were in the honeymoon phase – with a clear idea of what we wanted to accomplish and how to get there. But as time progressed, I noticed that I was carrying the majority of the weight. The workload would become uneven and I would work tirelessly to pick up the slack.

It came to the point that I'd question whether our partnership was even worth it. I was running myself into the ground and not getting the same amount of time and energy back from my partners. This is when I turned to my husband for advice, and what he made me realise helped catapult me to where I am today.

He showed me what he had seen in me all those years, and that is a woman who was more than capable of venturing off and doing her own thing. He told me that he saw a fearless, driven and determined individual who just needed to take the leap. And so, I did. One day, I decided to put my foot down. I parted ways with my partners and pursued my long overdue dream of building up my own company.

This reinvention took a lot of courage. I had to dig deep in myself and see all the great things that could come out of it. However, I learned it was not as easy as just speaking it into the universe. Change requires action, and I quickly decided to take it.

**

In this period of reinvention, I learned many things.

DO NOT BE RULED BY FEAR

Fear has the power to limit people and stop them from reaching their full potential. I was overrun by fear; fear that I wouldn't be able to make it on my own, fear of failure, fear of the unknown. However, I came to find that, once I stopped fearing negative outcomes and started embracing the possibility of success, the ball was in my court.

Like the game of tennis – which was my first love – when you step onto the court, it is up to you to hit the ball or let it go past you. With courage, you must learn to look fear in the eye, own your strengths and take your shot. Because if you don't take action, there is no growth for yourself and your business.

With this comes the harsh reality of things not going your way. When this happens, you might think your loss is a failure. However, it is extremely important to realise that it is so much more than that – it is a lesson. It's through our failures that we are able to elevate. As humans and business owners, the more that we learn, the more we grow.

In times of reinvention, especially when it comes to business, you must learn to trust the process. A life coach of mine once shared that you are always in the right place, at the right time and with the right people. This is something that I carry with me every day of my life, and it helps me understand that whatever happens – both good and bad – is meant to happen for a reason.

When reinventing, know that fear is normal but the power it holds on you is yours to determine.

YOU ARE HUMAN

As hard as we try to strive for perfection, we are bound to fail. As humans, we are hardwired in a way that being perfect is impossible. Failure, whether we like it or not, is a constant force in our lives. Though it is easier said than done, when things don't go our way (especially in reinvention) we have to take it as it is, learn from it and grow.

In business, you will face obstacles that may seem impossible to overcome. But one thing I learned is that we have the power to continue on. As business owners, we must be driven by the purpose our business serves. Focus on your company's *why*, as it will give you the power to carry on, even when times get tough.

In addition to this, I learned that we are never alone. We have so many mentors that we can run to, it's just a matter of reaching out to them and asking the right questions. More often than not, they will be happy to help. Reinvention can be a tricky thing, it is always a good idea to seek advice, opinions and insights from others.

I am a firm believer that teamwork makes the dream work, and I speak from experience when I say it truly does.

I know for a fact that good habits help create a great future. In all my years of business, this is something that I have held dear every day. I learned early on that if you are able to create positive and meaningful habits, there is no limit to how far you can go.

These habits don't have to be major habits. They can be punctuality for meetings, putting in a little extra effort in appearance so that you feel your best or something as small as being grateful for the life you lead and the business you run. These are just some of the many habits that I have developed along the years, and they have helped me tremendously.

Building the right habits may seem like a small task, but it can definitely take you a long way, both in business and in life.

KNOW YOUR *WHY*

Knowing your purpose can help you and your business grow immensely. Without it, the company simply cannot start. When it comes to your business, you have to ask yourself these questions:

- Why am I here?
- What do I want to accomplish?
- What is my purpose?
- How can I execute this?

Once these are established, use the answers you formulate as fuel to drive your business in the direction it needs to be. Your *why* is the foundation of everything that your company does and should be emphasised accordingly. A strong *why* can carry your business to great heights. If used correctly, there are no limits to what you can achieve.

My company's *why* was built on a passion to help elevate others and their businesses to reach greater heights. I developed this with these simple steps:

- Determine what you want to do.
- Clarify who you want to help.
- Plan out how to go about it.
- Take action.

Once these have been set, the possibilities are endless.

Think of your business as a car. A car needs gas to move, otherwise it will stay in its place. In this sense, your *why* would be the gas and your business would be the car. Your *why* fuels your business and helps it move. Without a purpose, your business will stay stagnant, and you don't want that. So, build your *why* and make it as powerful as can be because it plays a vital role in the success of your business.

With a clear purpose and the right mindset, anything is possible.

THERE IS ALWAYS TOMORROW

The reinvention process can get addicting. However, there is a lot that goes into reinventing a business. As much as we want it to happen overnight, the reality of it is it will be a long and tedious process.

With this, it is important that we remind ourselves to take it easy. There is always tomorrow. At times, I have to catch myself trying to finish everything in one day, and I have learned that it is impossible.

When it comes to your business, there are never-ending to-do lists. In the reinvention process, there are even more things that need to be done. But through all of this we must remember to draw the line and call it a day. Know your limits and know that it is okay to take care of yourself.

Self-love and self-care are not selfish. Allow yourself to rest, you deserve it.

INTEGRITY IS KEY

Integrity is a major driving force in how I live my life and how I run my business. By definition, it is the practice of being honest and showing a consistent and uncompromising adherence to strong moral and ethical principles and values. In ethics, integrity is regarded as the honesty and truthfulness or accuracy of one's actions.

One of the many pillars that hold my business up is integrity. I believe that it can make all the difference in how you operate. Throughout my reinvention process, I realised that integrity deals a lot with staying true to you and your business' *why*.

I learned that it is important for us to know and accept that we are not perfect. Despite the little voice in our heads telling us that we need to be, we are not perfect, and people don't expect us to be. The sooner we come to embrace the fact that we do not know everything, the faster we can lead our lives and businesses with integrity.

As cliché as it sounds, honesty is the best policy.

***

Once I took all of these factors and applied it in my reinvention, I saw an insane amount of potential in the vision I had for my business. Suddenly, the world was filled with endless opportunities for me to leave a positive mark. I just had to take action to make it happen.

Change is not always pretty. Oftentimes we get caught in the scariness of it all. But once we learn to trust the process and power through obstacles, there is no telling how far your business can go. You simply have to take the leap and go for it.

As I reinvented myself and my business, I'd think back to my childhood years as an athlete. I remember running track and the thrill it gave as I waited for the gunshot to be fired, signalling us to go. I also remembered feeling extremely nervous before every race, anxious that the outcome would not be in my favour. But, in the short moments that lead to the gunshot, I would gather all of my courage, muster up every bit of energy I had and go for gold. This is exactly what we need to do in business when reinventing. We don't always see it, but we have power to take that leap, make the change and succeed.

Reinvention is what you make it to be. Make it great.

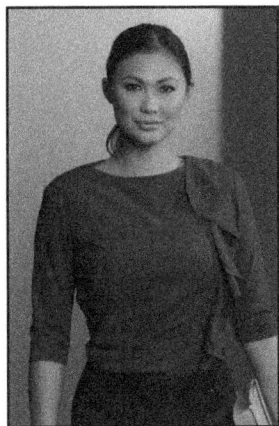

MAFAE YUNON-BELASCO

Maria Rafaela 'Mafae' Yunon-Belasco is best known for her success in the beauty pageant industry, having won prestigious awards locally and internationally, such as Miss Philippines Australia 1998, Binibining Pilipinas World 2003 (and prominently landing top five in the Miss World competition of the same year held in Sanya, China) and Mrs Philippines Globe 2008.

She has since gone on to channel her expertise into image consulting for Binibinig Pilipinas (Miss Philippines Pageant) since 2003, taking on the role of personality development director for the Miss World Philippines in 2021 and pageant director of Kumu Global Pageants on the number one live streaming app of the Philippines, Kumu. She continued on in her journey in expanding her services and entrepreneur expertise, starting up her own company, Mafae Management Consultancy (founded 2015), wherein she manages talents, spearheads public relations and marketing, content creation, events management, online show production and social media management for companies and individuals all over the world.

Mafae has vast experience in commercial, ramp and print modelling, and even television and events hosting. She enjoys passing on her knowledge of each of her experiences through her talks, workshops and shows, which she does on a weekly basis. She is firm in her mission of making the world a brighter space as a certified life and personality development coach, sacred space holder and wellbeing boost facilitator wherein she helps others become their best selves through positive mindset guidance.

Mafae, alongside her husband Nic Belasco, former professional basketball player in the PBA (Philippine Basketball Association), also owns a sports academy – the Belasco Unlimited Skills Academy where she coaches tennis. Mafae is passionate about empowering others with her family campaign #SaveLivesOnline, where she encourages others to be their true and authentic selves online while populating the digital world with positive content.

Recently, she was awarded 100 Most Influential Filipino Women on LinkedIn 2021, took on the roles of Australian regional director and Kumu creators' academy head for Kumu.

Mafae lives by her motto 'the world is yours' and 'time + productivity = success', and aims to bring the best out of everyone around her.

Lastly, the biggest reward in her life is being a mum, bringing up her own young leaders of today in her six children, Nico, Mike, Moses, Nicole, Noah and Melo. To add the cherry on top is her husband Nic, who supports and mentors Mafae in all that she does.

Website: mafaemanagement.com

EMPOWER YOURSELF

Marika Gare

INTRODUCTION

Making the decision to become an entrepreneur and start your own business takes a huge leap of faith, but it's also the most amazing decision you will make. Following your dream and accomplishing all you set out to do brings the greatest sense of accomplishment, allowing you to discover who you really are and what you are capable of. It forces you to continually evaluate yourself and to find that freedom and happiness we all crave.

BE PASSIONATE

> *'Be fearless in the pursuit of what sets your soul on fire.'*

The most important thing when starting a business is to make sure the idea you are building on is your absolute true passion. When you follow your heart's true desire, it increases your chance of success, because you are following your soul's desire and purpose.

For me, I always wanted to start my own business and be my own boss. Working over the years, I learnt that I enjoy working autonomously and this was my happy place in work as I could follow my own intuition and ideas, and just knuckle down and get stuff done. I spent years putting in the extra yards, really engaging myself in the whole business, not just the position I was involved in. This gave me the confidence I knew all factors of the business and could provide an ultimate service that I became known for. I couldn't stand the thought of not being able to assist someone or not knowing the answer to a question, so I was constantly evolving myself to ensure I could fulfil anything that came my way. Knowledge is power.

So, the desire to start my own business came when I realised how miserable I was with the whole groundhog day routine, I wasn't being acknowledged for my hard work and I had no sense of enjoyment. I saw an advert in the paper one day, advertising for someone to assist with personal organisation at an hourly rate. It made me think, *Why couldn't this be done for the type of work I do?* At this point in time, virtual assistants (VAs) were unheard of in Perth, Western Australia. So, I set about researching and found that while there were businesses that offered remote work over east and across the country, there wasn't really anything much in Perth. This gave me the excitement that perhaps I could follow my dream of starting my own business and build the life I had always dreamed of.

I spent the next two years researching, following online business communities, reading up on business processes, training myself in programs and brainstorming ideas for my business. Every time I thought about it, I felt an excitement I hadn't felt in a long time, I just knew I had to follow this path.

Fast forward two years later, I found myself heavily pregnant and still plodding along in a job that didn't satisfy me. When redundancies were offered at work, I jumped at the opportunity as this could fund my dream. At first, it was not accepted as they didn't want to lose me, but I was also preparing to bring a child into this world on my own (a story for another time) and I needed to provide for us. The thought of doing it all alone was very overwhelming, but I would not allow myself to miss the first few years with my baby just to return to work in a job I was miserable in. The most precious and important thing in the world is a soul you create.

I spent the first ten months after my son was born learning how to be a new mum and enjoying everything it brings. After this time, funds were getting low, and I realised it was time to bring some finances in. I made the decision it was time to start my dream and build my business. Of course, my family and friends thought I was nuts and advised me to get a 'real job' where I could have financial security and constant income for my child and myself, but I just couldn't. I would not allow myself to go back to a life I was miserable in. I had to follow my dream, I knew I could do it and if I didn't give it a chance, I would always regret it.

My desire, passion and sheer determination are what encouraged me to continue. I would not give up until I had what I wanted and could be self-sufficient in providing for us. That was important to me, and to be happy doing it.

I put my son in day care two days a week and started giving purpose to my passion. I came up with a plan, a strategy, built on it and prepared myself mentally for the challenges ahead. I had a vision board, watched inspirational videos, read books on business journeys and thought about it every moment. You have to be your own best supporter sometimes, and I wanted to show everyone I could do it. I could follow my dream, it was worthy of my time, and I would not only do it, but I'd become one of the best. I hate being told to dampen my dreams. No way!

RISING FROM THE ASHES TO BECOME THE PHOENIX

'And just as the phoenix rose from the ashes, she too will rise. Returning from the flames, clothed in nothing but her strength, more beautiful than before.' – Shannen Heartz

For many of us, life gives us challenges to face in many different forms – relationships, health issues, death, pain. It is how we grow as a person, how we determine our success in life and how we discover ourselves.

It also provides insight as to how we engage in business and navigate through hurdles, becoming conscious of yourself and your responses.

I was diagnosed with Crohn's disease at age fourteen and was told my life would never be normal again. I had my first bowel resection at fifteen and died on the operating table (well for a short moment, obviously I'm still here!). Not long afterwards, I lost both my grand-fathers a month apart – two men I absolutely adored and looked up to so much. I lost my brother when I was twenty-six which rocked me to my core and shook apart the way I saw everything in this world. I chose relationships I lost myself in and weren't good for my soul, I served others more than I served myself to gain approval. I watched my father battle multiple brain tumours, each time not knowing what the outcome would be or if he would survive. I endured and survived a major car crash at the age of thirty-four that resulted in internal inju-ries, facial surgery and severe head and brain trauma. I lost 70% of my memory, had to train my brain how to talk again, had long-term phys-ical rehab to learn to stand and walk without falling over, never really knowing if I would succeed or if my brain would ever fully recover. It took three years for my brain to get back to full capacity. I suffered anxiety and PTSD, some days not being able to leave the house as the anxiety was so overwhelming. I had limited use of my left arm and could barely dress myself, let alone wash my hair. A few years later I had my second bowel resection, became pregnant against all odds, and became a new mother on my own.

At the time I was going through all these things, I thought, *How will I get through this? Why me? What have I done to deserve this?* I felt like I was being punished. But the universe was preparing me for greater things.

I say this because you can either choose to lie down and let life tumble over you, leaving you defeated and broken, or you can rise to the challenge and say, *Not today, I will not be defeated! I deserve to live this life and I deserve to have dreams and follow them.* Learn from your experiences and use them as tools to grow stronger.

So many people live through horrible traumas or life-changing events, they're always extremely difficult, but it could be worse. I am always grateful for what I have. I didn't lose any limbs or my eyesight, I was able to complete rehab and train myself back again. Some people don't get that chance, I wanted to push through to live the life others would not be able to. I feel I have a responsibility to do that. I'm a survivor.

One thing I can say without a doubt is that starting regular meditation was life-changing for me. It calmed my mind, alleviated the stress and PTSD, gave me focus and clarity and allowed me to awaken my soul once more.

I see my car accident as a blessing in disguise which people think I'm crazy for saying. But I was forced to build myself from the ground up again, to discover what's important to me, to fight for myself and my health, to change the direction my life was going and to follow my dreams by igniting my awareness and soul's purpose. What did I want out of life? Was I on the right path to do that? How could I change things so I am more aligned with my heart's desire and live a life I am insanely happy in?

I gave myself a five-year plan. I wanted to get back to full health (physically and mentally), I wanted to buy a house, I wanted to start my own business, I wanted children and I wanted to be happy with my life every day, to have wonderful friends around me and spend time with those I love. To continue my soul's journey and bring my intuition and guidance into everyday life.

I use the strength I harnessed during these times every day, I find my quiet inner mind through meditation whenever I have a stressful moment or situation, I ask for guidance, I set my intentions and make changes to fulfil those intentions. I have a vision board to keep my goals in mind, I find three things I am grateful for every morning before I get out of bed and I never lose hope.

If you can find a positive in each challenging situation, you can understand how to use it as a tool to improve yourself or your business. Engage in making everything the best version it can be. Because … why not? What are you waiting for? Why not be the best version of you? Or make your business the best it could be?

No matter how incredibly hard these things are, once you come out the other side, you realise how strong you are, that you can rise again. Nothing is impossible, everything has a solution, you just need to find what that is and work on it.

Evolve from the ashes and become the phoenix of your own legend.

MAKE THE MOST OUT OF WHAT YOU HAVE

'You were meant to be here right now, so make the most of it.'
– Ken Poirot

So, going back to when I started my business … being out of work for almost a year with no income, my funds – I will admit – were really low. Starting a business with a high mortgage and a baby on my own with little money and on absolutely no sleep did sound absurd. But like I said, if I really want something I will stop at nothing to get it and if it all falls apart, then the universe is telling me this is not my path, and I will accept what I must do.

But you know when you get those random things happen and it all just works with the idea you have been thinking of or the path you want to follow, and you know you're on the right track? Well, that's how I knew the universe would support me in my new adventure.

Being low on finances, I needed to find a way to make it work. What essentials did I need to get started? I needed a laptop and internet (der!), procedures, a website, service agreements, marketing ideas and avenues to find clients. I researched the best laptop for my requirements and asked everyone to pitch in as a birthday present. Done. I joined the local library where I could use free internet any time I needed because I couldn't afford home internet. I also had the intention to hotspot internet from my phone to my laptop for times I wanted to work from home. I researched business plans, best processes, how to find clients, how to market, all the nitty-gritty new business owners need to know. I joined the NEIS program which is a government-funded program assisting those with great ideas to start a business. They taught the financials of starting a business, in-depth business plans, marketing tools and prepared us for the journey ahead. Once completed we got twelve months free business mentoring. Bonus. Done.

I spent my days reviewing businesses on social media, completing free courses, reading business books and preparing as much as possible for any obstacle that may come my way.

Of course, starting a business when you don't even have an office, let alone a computer, printer or home internet was challenging, but I made it work. And as money came in, I put it back into the business. I didn't splash out on a new home computer, printer or home internet for at least a year or more. I utilised all I could for the free or cheaper version. Do what you need to do to make it happen. I don't agree with obstacles, I just work on it until I find a solution. You don't get anywhere without hard work, and I had the determination to get there.

Don't get me wrong, I still have days when I'm feeling a little low and that's normal, life isn't always roses and you'd be pretty soulless if nothing ever got to you. But if you make the most out of each moment, each opportunity, each stage in your life, you will be able to master staying positive and harnessing that intention of great things.

WORKING THROUGH CHALLENGES

'Often it's the deepest pain which empowers you to grow into your higher self.' – Karen Sahansohn

The best way to start the process is to work out why it is a challenge (apart from the obvious) for you personally. Psychoanalyse the situation and your response to it. Once you are aware of how it makes you feel and why, you can work on how best to approach it.

Throughout our lives we experience many things both good and bad, but it is how we react to those experiences that shapes us as a person and how we deal with situations in all areas of our lives. Knowing yourself and your behaviour gives great insight to use in business. Nobody tells you starting a business is just as much a personal journey as it is a business one.

I knew when I started my business that I didn't have much confidence in myself as a business owner, especially being new and still learning the ropes. I tended to hide in the background. Yes, I had an insatiable desire and passion for what I was doing, I'd done a ton of research and preparation, but I hadn't considered that marketing my business was about promoting *me*. I had no idea how to promote myself, what made me stand out from the crowd? I worked in the background and got things done. But what could I offer on a personal level? What brand did I want my business to have? How do others see me and my brand? What did I want to achieve from my conversations? Who was I as a businessperson?

I was painfully shy and anxious in big groups, but I craved the discussions and support of other entrepreneurs, so I knew I had to get myself out there and throw myself in it. I joined a networking group, pushing myself to work through the anxiety, and over time I became less of an introvert and more confident in myself as a business owner, learning how to promote myself and build those relationships with others. Being an entrepreneur, you are your business, and while I know I am good at what I do, this wasn't previously coming across in my dealings with people as I wasn't showing that confidence.

Something that has always helped me is having three preparations:

Plan A – the best possible outcome for the situation.

Plan B – the back-up plan if it all goes to sh*t.

Plan C – the totally unexpected.

Put plans and procedures in place for all of them and you will rarely find yourself in a situation you are not prepared for.

BE CREATIVE AND INTUITIVE

'Intuition is seeing with the soul.' – Dean Koontz

Over time, I've learnt to bring my creative side into my business and work with my intuition to aid with my choices and confidence. As women, sometimes we suppress this side of ourselves as we feel it needs to be one or the other. I'm either a business professional or I'm a caring intuitive friend/mother etc.

I have always loved being creative but didn't feel it fit with promoting me as a professional. I began doing what I loved outside of work first – painting, sketching, drawing – then decided I could use this creativity and my love for exploring new things and turn it into something more for my clients. So, I began practising and playing around with ideas, and when clients wanted me to create graphics for them, I was in my element. I could create, develop content, produce something I loved doing and get paid for it.

I am also intuitive in choosing my clients. Yes, *choosing.* Just because they come to you for work, does not mean it would be a great fit and sometimes the challenges and stress it brings trying to work with two different personalities isn't worthwhile. It affects your stress levels both in and out of work, and these days, I prefer to do what makes my soul happy. Being around amazing people who appreciate you as a person and a business owner and acknowledge and praise the effort you put in is what makes us all happy. And it brings an even greater desire to help their business be at it's optimum because you love working with them and you want them to succeed just as much as they do.

SUMMARY

Provide yourself with a sense of empowerment through knowledge, ignite your awareness and understanding and harness your soul's true desire.

MARIKA GARE

Marika Gare grew up in Perth and is the multi-award-winning owner and founder of Perth Virtual Services, providing small and medium businesses with business solutions.

She shares her knowledge and wisdom with other business owners, encouraging them to awaken the full potential of their business, assisting them to navigate through obstacles and bring their goals to fruition.

Having a highly successful business herself and having worked with such a variety of other business owners, she shares what she has learnt from her personal journey to help them optimise their business.

Marika is mother to a beautiful son, who inspires her every day to be a better mother, person and business owner. The love for her child is the reasoning behind everything she does, providing solid foundations, showing him resilience and passion, and encouraging him to follow dreams.

PURPOSE

When positivity and problem-solving
are a superpower
Melissa Haque

It's a really exciting time when you're in the planning stages of launching a business. It's all still the theory of an idea, you're putting plans in place that you think should work and you hope will happen.

Launching a business doesn't happen overnight, it's a journey and takes true determination as the work is hard with long hours. So, to set yourself up for success, time needs to be spent planning and building out your business strategy. Even if your plan is forever changing, the benefit is in the journey as it forces you to sit and really think about what you want, what you can do and where you want to go with your idea. It's also one of the things that is often left till last when starting a business, particularly if it's a product-based business as you've been so busy creating and designing your products that there hasn't been much time for anything else.

Throughout my business journey I've made many mistakes and learnt many lessons. Trust me when I say that life in business is easier when you have a plan and back yourself. It allows you to navigate the many challenges that come your way, but also shines light on the opportunities.

156

From navigating imposter syndrome and endless hours of mama-guilt whilst juggling my family, a corporate career and growing my business, I've been able to find the gold nuggets of success and really lean into opportunities presented during the tough times. People constantly ask me how I juggle it all and how I am always so positive, so to help set you up for success, I'm sharing five ways I've been able to keep my positive outlook and grow my business into what it is today. I'll be covering:

1. Why your business needs to light you up.
2. What to consider when pricing your product.
3. The art of collaborating with others to create awareness without the cost.
4. How to use technology to create efficiency from the start.
5. Where to find your courage to make big decisions.

IT NEEDS TO LIGHT YOU UP

You can't build a business in a day, a week or a month; it takes time, patience and a lot of hard work. Both my parents are serial entrepreneurs and have owned, run and built businesses that I've been part of my whole life. When I was a kid, every school holidays were spent with my family, and because my parents always worked for themselves, a lot of our family time meant working together in the family business. This is why I was so determined to forge a strong career working for someone else, and never had the desire to have my own business – I've seen how hard it can be. The long hours, the many hats you need to wear, the endless to-do lists and a nonstop busy mind and sleepless nights thinking about money. Just like the packet of Tim Tams that never runs out, well, for a business owner, it's a to-do list that never runs out.

Don't think I'm trying to scare you off before you start here, because there is obviously a reason I have landed where I am – but I wanted to make it clear that running a business is hard work and it will take everything in you to make it work. So ... after knowing this my whole life, and building a successful corporate career as a strategic marketer, why on earth would I walk away from it to run my own business?

Simple. It lights me up. Sometimes I smile so hard whilst strategising our next steps that I feel my cheeks starting to hurt. I am genuinely excited about my product, what it means for mamas and families and that I get to build, plan and execute my own business strategy every day.

When I started Wild Dough, I had just had my second child and felt lost when my job changed to being a stay-at-home mother to look after my toddler and newborn. I loved going to work each day. Some people need to stretch their legs and head out on a run each day, well, for me, my happy place is stretching my mind. I'm an expert at solving problems, coming up with strategies to sell something new or a new way to sell something. So, after I created a perfect playdough that was a lifesaver for our family, I just HAD to share it to help our other families like mine, even though I knew I would be stepping into entrepreneur land (you know, that place where I vouched I would never go). Being a mother is the hardest job in the world, and I had a product that could really help make life a little easier. Wild Dough had helped my family so much I felt so strongly toward wanting to help others who were just like me. So, there is my *why* – and even knowing how bloody hard it is to run your own business, I had finally found something that I felt so much stronger about.

It just so happened that in order to do this and create a successful business, I needed to do the things I loved to do in my corporate job; problem-solving, planning, building and executing strategies. So, as my worlds combined, working late nights, weekends and doing all the jobs I loved to do, plus the ones I didn't so much (ahem, bookkeeping), it has all felt worth it.

Before you launch your business, make sure you spend some time mapping out what it is you love to do, what is your mission and purpose for your business and how you think you might make it happen. If you're up all night strategising with excitement and can't keep the smile off your face, then this is likely right for you. If it's already causing more stress and anxiety than you're comfortable with but you haven't even launched yet, then maybe this isn't THE idea you need to run with. There will be another tomorrow and the next day, I assure you, perhaps you're still waiting for the right one.

KNOW YOUR NUMBERS — PRICE FOR PROFIT

For creative businesses that make or manufacture their own products it's a difficult decision to know what to charge, especially if it's a unique product or you're in an unsaturated industry. It's also one of the most common mistakes that product businesses make as there are a lot of things to consider when understanding the costs that go into your product.

Pricing is one of my initial mistakes, in fact, it only took me three months to realise I had underpriced our initial jar offering. I had worked for so long to ensure our recipe and product was perfect, and then worked on our packaging and brand identity, who and how to sell it to that I had neglected a pretty important piece – the price. At the time there was only a handful of handmade playdough businesses, all of which were quite different from mine and the direction I wanted to take so it was difficult to understand what the market would potentially pay for my product. Plus, I was riddled with imposter syndrome and wondering if anyone out there would actually buy my product, so I found this process really difficult. I worked out all the costs of ingredients and materials that went into our product, so I thought I had a baseline of what it was costing me. I used that figure as my starting point for all of our pricing without realising I had made the biggest business blunder of all. I had forgotten to include the price of time and hadn't factored in any labour for the making of our product – quite the blunder considering Wild Dough is handmade and labour is now the biggest cost that goes into it.

I smile now, thinking that I undervalued my own time so much. It wasn't deliberate neglect but rather inexperience that led me to do this. Once I realised we needed to increase our retail price, I made sure I announced the price rise and clearly communicated it to my customers, including when it would happen to allow them a last chance to purchase at the current rates.

Since then, our retail pricing hasn't changed, however we constantly have needs to work out specific pricing as we have partnered with large corporations to stock our product as well as tendered for other large orders. Knowing our numbers has been key to being able to profitably grow and successfully partner with so many different organisations that purchase our product. I've built a large spreadsheet that I continually update that includes all of our base costs of materials and ingredients as well as labour requirements for certain volumes. I input the required volume of product and the spreadsheet calculates all of my base costs including materials and ingredients plus allows me to work out labour costs based on time. It's helped us price, be ready to procure and also understand time frames for large orders. I'm more of a creative than mathematician, but this is one part of the business process that is so important to get right, so even if it's not your forte, it's important to spend time and energy understanding what your numbers are.

Here's some things I've done to help me keep track and properly price our product offering:

- List our all your materials/ingredients (including packaging) and their costs, using the same unit for each of them.
- Work out the price of labour you'd like to pay and factor it in (whether you pay it to yourself from the start, or just have it factored in for the future, if your product is handmade this is really important).
- Build a simple spreadsheet and use some basic formulas to identify the cost and cost for volume.
- Save your spreadsheet using online software like Dropbox, office.com or Google Sheets as this will allow you to access it from anywhere.

- Understand what economies of scale will do for your pricing and the positive impacts.

THE ART OF COLLABORATION

Have you ever wondered how some people launch a business and it just goes *BOOM*? It makes immediate sales and just seems to take off? It looks like they have an endless marketing budget and have hired some pros to work for them. What if I told you I launched Wild Dough in September and that in October I had my first five-figure month in sales, and we were selling a $7.50 product at the time, with absolutely no advertising spend?

When I started Wild Dough, I was new to the small business social community world. I didn't have a thriving Instagram account, in fact, I started with zero followers. I didn't understand Facebook ads and didn't have the budget to hire an expert to help me. But having a background in marketing, I knew that I needed to create some awareness and cast my net to capture potential customers. I knew my product was superior, but I needed a way to tell everyone so they stopped to listen and take notes. As I was brand new, no-one followed me or knew me, why would they listen when I told them that my product was great? Well, I didn't tell them that. In fact, instead of growing my own following, I spent all my time and effort looking for accounts to collaborate with, so they could endorse Wild Dough and share how great it was to their own communities.

As I had a clear understanding that I was selling to parents, and in particularly mothers, I went searching for a community of accounts that were sharing content targeting this group. And wasn't I surprised to know there are A LOT of them! So, I started creating a list of accounts that I would love to collaborate with.

A collaboration arrangement can look many different ways, but the way I did it at the start was to offer the account I was collaborating with a generous amount of my product in exchange for photos and a shout-out

161

of my product on their own social platform (usually Instagram). I would reach out and share a little about my story and my mission for Wild Dough. I would always say to share an honest review and would never influence what I hoped they would say.

I remember the day that I reached out to a beautiful play account on Instagram with seventy thousand followers. I had been following her for a while and desperately wished to see my products amongst the other gorgeous ones she supported but was so afraid of reaching out that I didn't for weeks. Then, finally, I reminded myself what was the worst that could happen and sent the message I'd drafted days before. When she replied with a yes, I was beside myself and jumped around the house with excitement. I send her the most beautiful box of Wild Dough which she shared to her network and also became a long-term supporter.

Using this collaboration method, I never spent any money on advertising, I merely exchanged product in return for awareness and endorsement within their own established communities. In return, my following grew, people became aware of Wild Dough as many accounts they followed were continually endorsing it and became customers of mine. It also meant that I had a steady stream of gorgeous photos coming in that I could use to share to my own Instagram page, featuring these wonderful influencers I was working with, ensuring instant social proof and credibility of my brand.

It never gets any easier, as I recently reached out to an account with 700,000 followers and held my breath for two days waiting for their reply. It helped that she already knew of me and was familiar with my brand as I'd been interacting with her. I reminded myself the worst that could happen is that she says 'no' and went for it.

My top tips on starting your own collaborations:
- Find accounts who have a following of your target customer, these could be on any form of social media, blogs or even podcasts.
- Start a list of accounts you would love to work with.

- Start engaging with these accounts, follow them, like and comment on their posts.
- Reach out via DM or email and ask! When you ask, share your *why*, be personable, relatable and be clear on your offer, but also be ready and happy to negotiate.
- Make sure you document your agreement and make it clear as to what both parties agree to.
- Remember, no matter the size of the account, there is another human behind it, just like you, so be brave and shoot them that message. What's the worst that could happen?

SAVING TIME WITH TECHNOLOGY

When I launched Wild Dough I had a full-time corporate career, my husband worked shifts most weekends and many nights PLUS we had two children under three. I was also already suffering heavily from mama-guilt, as I was busy focusing a sum of energy on launching this business when I felt I should be focusing it all on my family. People always wonder how on earth I was able to do all those things and grow my business on the side. How could I spend time with my family, mother my young children, keep moving forward in my corporate careers and keep taking Wild Dough from strength to strength? The answer is it hasn't been easy, but I like to think of myself as the queen of efficiency. I am constantly looking for easier ways to do things.

At the start, before I had budget for staff or outsourcing, I would spend multiple hours every night working on my social media content and interacting with the community. I'd barely sleep as then I'd spend hours on customer service, making our product, packaging it and packing orders. I will never forget that first Christmas that I handwrote the name and address on four hundred parcels before I figured out a better way to do it.

Over time, I have implemented so many systems using really handy technology that have allowed me to make all the time I spend on the business as efficient as possible. This has given me space to spend time with my children and family, and at the start, allowed me space to continue my corporate career. And then, as Wild Dough expanded, I've been able to use these same systems with my staff and be confident in knowing they're working efficiently too. Most importantly, this meant the time I spend working is time working ON the business, instead of IN the business.

I've tried and tested many ways to improve our processes and efficiency and here are some ways to use technology that have been transformational to our business and saving time:

- Ecommerce store. By building my online store using Shopify I was able to integrate my social, ads, payments and shipping altogether quite easily. I even built my website myself as it's a low-cost, simple-to-use platform and best in class for product-based businesses.

- Social media posting. By using a program to plan and automatically post my social media content I no longer need to stare blankly at the screen wondering what I'm going to post and take time away from my family, as peak posting time usually corresponds with dinner at our house. It also keeps me organised as I just need to block out two hours of time each week to write and plan what is coming up and schedule them for posting to ensure I never miss a day. There are so many apps and programs out there that can be used to do this so find one that suits you and will post to the social platforms that you use.

- Customer service. It's so important to be able to respond to customers quickly, however, it's often difficult keeping track of all the details and I found we continually needed to check multiple systems to find orders and postage tracking information. We implemented software by Gorgias to bring all of this together which has cut down the time we spend on customer service by half.

- Shipping. Sending products to customers is a huge process within itself, and a costly one at that. By using a shipping software in conjunction with our online Shopify store we've been able to compare a number of couriers to identify the lowest cost for each parcel as well as print shipping labels at the push of a button.

• Design. From email design to social media posts and advertising images, design is required so frequently. We use Canva, a free design software, to manage all of this in one place meaning we never have to wait for a designer again as we can easily edit and update images on the go. Many software options also now let you remove the background from images and therefore is our new best friend when it comes to product photography, particularly for websites.

BACK YOURSELF – FIND YOUR COURAGE

My oldest friend has described me as 'fearless' many times over the years, which I absolutely adore and aspire daily to be so. But in truth, I don't feel fearless at all, in fact, I'm probably more afraid of failure than the average person. I think what makes me appear fearless is that I'm a problem-solver – I do things that others may not, because I know I'll be able to find a way. I trust that if I say I can do something, I will do it and be able to make it work. Then, in the instance that it doesn't work as originally planned, I go back to the drawing board and figure out another way to make it happen.

There's no such thing as failure, there's only success or a lesson. When feeling afraid to do something (and I will tell you, it happens on a daily basis) I first ask myself, *What's the worst that can happen?*

Fear of failure comes in many forms and levels, especially if there is a large expense involved. If you fail, it's not just pride on the line, it's also savings. The biggest hurdle I've had to overcome was in our second year of business when the COVID-19 pandemic started in 2020. My hometown of Melbourne (which ended up earning notoriety for holding the longest lockdown in the world) rolled out very strict lockdown rules. At the time, Wild Dough was based out of my home, I had a purpose-built room where Wild Dough was made and staff came to my house. It really was a perfect working-from-home scenario until these new rules meant people weren't allowed in homes and manufacturing had to close. This led us into a situation where it was impossible to keep up with demand without staff to help and we ended up closing for four months with no stock. This really spiralled me to business rock bottom, I was so disheartened, my interstate family was locked out, my corporate job had been restructured and my business had been forced to scale right back to near closing. I like to think I'm a specialist at problem-solving but this was a situation I found it very hard to figure myself out of.

I kept going back to one thing, and one thing alone. My product is great and I backed it 100%. I knew that my product was superior, it had helped me, we had hundreds of loyal customers who kept coming back again and again as they felt the same, so I just needed to figure out a way to be able to get my staff back and reopen the business and the sales would come.

I laid all my ideas out on the table then realised I needed some help with this, so I reached out to my network. I let them pour into my courage cup as they told me I'd be able to do this. I asked my family for their support, and they helped shield me from the fear that was stopping me taking the next step. I undertook a risk analysis to ensure I understood what I needed to do vs. the risks if it didn't work out.

Then I took the plunge. I decided I was going to expand my business, and within the week, I had leased a warehouse that I wasn't able to go and see due to the lockdown. I had meetings in place regarding our launch into the United States. I had hired my first staff member.

Three weeks later we were back up and running in our first headquarters outside of my home with my new team in place. We did a huge production run and sent our first pallet of jars to the USA to a warehouse to sell directly there. We opened back up to the Australian market.

Two months later our business sales were four times more than our best month ever before.

I never knew if taking the leap, the risk and the plunge would work out for me. But after I had understood all the risks, planned out what I needed to do and filled my courage cup to the top with the help and support of my family, I knew it was a leap I had to take. And it was worth it.

Next time you need to find some more courage, try some of the things that have helped me:

- Make a list of pros and cons or do a risk/cost analysis. When you fully understand the risks involved, it's easier to plan ways to overcome them. Try and break it down to smaller bite-size chunks as it always seems less scary this way.
- Talk to your cheer squad. This may be your own social community, your family, a mentor or friends. Find those people that will be your biggest supporters and involve them in your journey when you need some encouragement or a different point of view and let them pour into your courage cup – you aren't the only one who can fill it.
- Ask yourself what is the worst that can happen and understand what is holding you back. Is it pride, fear or something else? And focus your energy on understanding and then overcoming this.

Don't give up, just modify.

MELISSA HAQUE

Known for her passion for business, cheerful disposition and overly loud laugh, Melissa Haque is an award-winning entrepreneur, business mentor, marketing maven and mother.

As founder and chief of leading playdough brand Wild Dough, Melissa is on a mission to give mothers the tools, education and the products to facilitate exciting sensory experiences for their children, whilst claiming some time back for themselves.

Wild Dough is a playdough like no other as it was developed specifically for little hands. Melissa created it for her own daughter after tiring of the generic playdough tubs continually drying out and never being soft enough for her two-year-old daughter to roll herself.

After an extensive amount of time searching for an alternative, Melissa took matters into her own hands. She perfected the playdough recipe by creating Wild Dough. It's incredibly soft, non-drying, great-smelling playdough that encourages hours of imaginative and sensory play.

Melissa has successfully scaled Wild Dough from initially working from her kitchen bench, to a factory leading up to ten staff with the capacity to produce up to ten thousand units per week. Wild Dough is proudly handmade in Melbourne and is stocked in specialty stores across USA and Australia.

Melissa is also passionate about supporting other women to succeed in business. She has drawn on her background in strategic marketing and own experience building the Wild Dough business, brand and manufacturing to mentor and coach other business owners wanting to launch and scale their own self-made product business.

Website: wilddoughco.com.au & melhaque.com
Instagram: @wilddough.co & @mel.haque

OWN WORST ENEMY

Natashia Telfer

Starting anything new is often a jump into the unknown – weighing up a series of calculated risks, researching the market, the financial forecasting, weighing up the commitment versus the sacrifices, the pros and cons. This is all the black-and-white of business. Yet, I guarantee you, the greatest challenge you will face is only found within the grey ... your own mindset.

I have faced horrible and toxic relationships, cancer, years of IVF, multiple miscarriages, postnatal depression, experienced terrible bosses, workplace politics and have gone on to start up a handful of businesses – and I can still confidently say mindset is key.

If you are reading this book, I suspect it's because you are driven and ready to take on the world. We all hope to leave the world a little better than we found it and hopefully make a positive impact in whatever it is that we choose to do in life. So how can we do that? All it takes is YOU.

NEGATIVE NANCY

Are you sure this business venture is a good idea? Is it financially viable or is it just a hobby? What if it all falls apart? Am I financially viable to kickstart this? Do I have what it takes? I can't lead people. I don't know the first thing about business. I can't possibly have a family and a career. I don't have the courage.

Any of this appearing true for you? Let me introduce you to Nancy.

Nancy ruins everything and never has anything productive to say. Do you know who I am talking about? She is that voice in your head, your awful inner critic, your negative self-talk, your internal dialogue ... your own worst enemy! Nancy is stopping you from achieving your full potential. Sounds silly, but hear me out. She is responsible for telling you you're too fat for the dress, you need all the concealer to cover up the dark circles under your eyes, that cute guy won't call you back, you will fail your exam, you do not deserve that work promotion and risking everything to start up a business is most definitely a bad idea. She always operates on the side of caution, but excessively, so it is debilitating to your growth, potential and self-worth. She tricks you into thinking she is keeping you safe. Nancy dampens your self-esteem, your confidence and productivity. You are essentially in a psychologically abusive relationship with yourself. Most of us would run for the hills if this behaviour was coming from a partner or an employee, but how can we run from ourselves?

I would confidently say I am an optimist, but Nancy has been front and centre for as long as I can remember. At the age of eighteen she told me that my cancer diagnosis was the universe's way of weeding me out. I started treatment and the narrative turned to Nancy telling me that I was defying the odds and the consequence of that would be my inability to have children, and this remained my mindset through six years of IVF and multiple miscarriages, reaffirming Nancy's grip on my reality. Now I bet as you just read that, you thought to yourself, *Is this woman crazy?* but that's Nancy at her finest. At twenty-nine my now business partner approached me to start up our company. I had all the doubt in the world, *Why me? I can't do this. I know nothing about running a business. What if I fail?* But I had committed to my business partner, so I persevered because I refused to let them down. Six years in, now I am the successful managing director of a multimillion-dollar company and that business partner is now my bestie, but even through all of that, Nancy still had her hold on me despite the success.

It wasn't until the age of thirty-five I realised Nancy has no idea what she is talking about. Her thoughts are uninformed and uneducated. If this is the case, why did I give her so much power? Who is she and what is her purpose? Once I began to ask these questions to my inner critic, I realised she was merely thoughts and feelings I was allowing myself to have. These feelings are not reality. They are not an observation. They are not fact. They are not how others perceive me. This realisation was a game changer to shifting my mindset and ultimately opening a whole new world.

LEVEL UP

Despite advice in the dozens of self-help books I've devoured, I've learnt in practice that Nancy cannot be banished. You can, however, set boundaries. This is not an easy feat. Nancy is like your shadow, always attached to you but only visible if you allow her to be. I found the best method is to acknowledge her, and in doing so, she loses some of the power she holds. Call her out. Name her. *My inner critic is Nancy.* Naming her allows you to separate the feelings from facts. Calling her out often allows you to realise what you thought was fact holds no merit. Then unexpectedly, all those thoughts and feelings you had holding you back fade away with Nancy. You become vulnerable and uncomfortable in this new and unknown space, then suddenly you realise Nancy was your barrier.

It's only now you can move forward in unchartered territory. When you allow it, those things you used to think were impossible are now a possibility. Your mindset shifts and life opens, but it is an inside job only you can do for yourself. Going into business for the first few years,

I allowed Nancy to reign. With Nancy in charge, business sailed along. Yes, it was successful, but it was also safe, always proceeding with caution and second-guessing myself. When I took over the reins from Nancy and was able to call her out, all facets of life improved astronomically. I gained the clarity to make decisions in business based on evidence and facts rather than feelings or thoughts. This allowed me to be confident in my decision-making. Change is always uncomfortable, but it is only in that space growth truly can occur. It is in this space I was able to triple the size of my management team, double employees and expand the services offered and move to a new space five times larger, simply by having a clearer perspective no longer skewed by Nancy which allowed me to believe in myself and give life a good hard go. Shift in mindset costs absolutely nothing yet the benefits are immeasurable.

Cue LEVEL UP status. We level up through each school grade and work roles. We level up through adolescence and adulthood. We level up partners and friendships. This is just a simple fact of life impacted with aging. Then when it comes to the internal level ups, like our mentality and level of self-care, it often remains stationary if we allow it. I've spent the first thirty-plus years of my life keeping myself small. I feared people would say I've changed. I didn't want to let people down by saying no or disagreeing. The facts are that I have changed, and allowing myself to personally level up, in turn allowed my company to level up in ways I could have never imagined.

So where does one start with levelling up? By going back to basics. In business, it's about going back to the fundamentals and my *why*. Why do I do what I do, and more importantly, am I still aligned to my *why*? For me, my *why* is about giving back. Providing a health care service that is truly client focused even if that means tearing down government red tape to advocate for systemic change. My drive for equality in care has not waivered. My next review of basics are my work priorities. These are my utility belt, my toolbox, my life source, and would you believe, none are money or profit focused.

So, what are my top three work priorities?
1. Balance and flexibility.
2. Perspective and growth.
3. Tribe and culture.

BALANCE AND FLEXIBILITY

Balance is my ultimate non-negotiable priority both personally and within the company. If one of my three work priorities is in jeopardy, it's usually an indication to me that I need to stop and re-evaluate what the company's current goals are because something is not aligned with my business mission. On the other hand, I am a self-confessed life-juggler and ball-dropper but that's where flexibility comes in. Flexibility in life and business is essential. Yes, there is a place for structure and routine, however, a flow of flexibility within your daily routine is where 'life' happens. I didn't anticipate getting cancer. I certainly did not anticipate suffering from postnatal depression (PND) after spending six years, multiple miscarriages and thousands and thousands of dollars on IVF. To then be diagnosed with PND, I had this additional layer of absolute guilt about having it (thanks, Nancy!). However, that is life. Sometimes your routine needs adjustment to stay the course and/or rerouting your course to survive.

It is with balance and flexibility, I believe *women can have it all.* There, I said it. We truly can, but 'all' does not come easy, and it does not come without sacrifice. Having it 'all' can look different to each of us and can evolve as we grow through different stages in our lives. For me, having it all is having my husband, my babies, my family, my friends, my health, having a balanced diet, seven hours sleep a night, a career, synergy within my company, a few dollars in my bank, a social life/activity of sorts and sunshine on my face at least once a week! The reality of having it 'all' is no one person can have all things at the one time. These things I value and consider my 'all' represent one of the many balls I juggle daily. Just as my business ball is reaching the top, often that means my friends ball is coming down and my social life ball might be on the ground rolling away from me, and I haven't seen my seven hours of sleep ball in weeks … but the point is, I have all those balls! It's up to me how much effort I put in and what I choose to keep up at the top. You can use this analogy even further just within business. As a one-woman show, you probably have a lot of juggling balls you are responsible for. When you start juggling too many balls and you feel the quality of your balls wavering, this is generally a good indication of growth within your business and a calling to recruit. Recruiting the right people to your circle at first may add balls to juggle while you go through the process of recruitment and induction, however, once that employee is onboard, you can begin to share your juggling balls, allowing you to concentrate on the balls you choose to hold, OR if you are like me, just making way for more balls to take on.

I always promote a work culture of balance and flexibility to my team where physically possible. We facilitate this with a self-directed workload approach. My casual team will dictate to me when they are available to work, and they are rostered accordingly. Those employees on permanent contracts have been offered these in consultation with the employee and on a 'flexibility is key' approach. Providing the true concept of balance and flexibility within the company has proven measurable in our employment retention. The team are actively supported to maintain a healthy work-life balance thus it becomes a win-win for all parties, after all, a happy team equals positive outcomes for clients and one less ball I am dropping today!

PERSPECTIVE AND GROWTH

Perspective and growth go hand-in-hand in business. In the early days I put in the sleepless nights and long hours as the roster clerk, the recruitment team, the advertisement team, the daily operational manager, the client relationships manager and governance overseer. I know maintaining all facets of a growing company will eventually become impossible, and unless something can change, that business is destined to fall over. Today, my business partner and I have been able to grow the team and share the load, with team players that excel in those specialised areas. Instead of me trying to control it all, I needed to implement a kickass team with the right skill sets to broaden the company scope. This freed me up to continue to grow the company. Perspective in growth is always remembering you are no better than any other person on your team. Each player is valuable and will in turn bring something to your team no other person can! Therefore, I still personally oversee the recruitment process to ensure our team players are more than just meeting the formal criteria, but they have the right attitude and common sense. Two things no résumé can ever tell me, and to be honest, if a résumé did tell me that, I wouldn't believe it!

In the workplace and in life, we all drop a ball or two every so often, and yes, sometimes those mistakes cost money. It's in these moments that perspective is paramount. Is the mistake going to matter in five minutes? Five hours? Five Days? Five weeks? If the answer is no to any of those questions, then let it go. The most important takeaway becomes owning the mistake and learning from it. Does there need to be a clearer process to outline the expectation or instruction? Or perhaps it was just human error too. The point is, it's perspective that will ensure you can remain a fair, compassionate and approachable company leader. Your team will know you will support them through the good and the bad, and that they can approach you with any problem without fear.

My perspective allows me to acknowledge and accept my company is often only a stepping stone for an employee. That is perfectly okay. There is a time and a space for every person you interact with in the business. Some are built for a short time, others a long time. This is always supported by our company approach of quality over quantity. Give me five amazing employees over fifty mediocre employees any day of the year!

This will effectively equate to five employees bringing in consistent and guaranteed income because they are highly sought after, opposed to fifty mediocre employees that may instantly inject my company with income at first, but would quickly and inevitably fizzle out when clients recognise the quality in service has diminished.

It is the amazing employees I choose to recruit; we also choose to invest in, foster growth and professional development for the team and myself. We have some phenomenal skill sets among our team they should be proud of and shared with the world and given the opportunity to utilise said skills wherever possible! For instance, one of our incredible employees is also an extraordinary cake maker. Where opportunity presents, you can bet we are singing her praises and booking-in cakes! Those incredible nursing student employees we hire who wear their heart on their sleeve – you can bet we will support them with grad-year application references. We want our team to kick all their goals because we keep things in check.

TRIBE AND CULTURE

'We are the average of the five people we spend the most time with.' This was famously said by motivational speaker Jim Rohn and relates to the law of averages. This is something I have kept in mind when creating my work tribe and culture. If we spend on average five days a week at work with colleagues, you can bet I am going to ensure they are kickass colleagues I select to employ. As I mentioned earlier, I still choose to oversee all recruitment to our tribe. The sole purpose of this is to ensure those we hire have aligning morals and values. Given my company is about people and care, it is paramount my employment style motives capture this. Essentially, by meeting with every qualified candidate and having an informal-style meeting, I can gauge the authenticity of the applicant. If that candidate was more interested in scoping out the office space and asking about pay rates straight off the bat, then this position probably isn't for them. I look for those I feel comfortable and at ease with. Those who will advocate for the rights of the clients and I envision contributing to team culture. I'm looking for employees who I would feel 110% comfortable in hiring to look after my own loved ones if ever needed.

Today our tribe is solid, and our culture is second nature. I credit this to our authentic approach with how we treat one another. Respectfully and with transparency. There is no visible hierarchy in our workplace. We all work side by side, there's no podiums at team meetings or stages at functions and there is no task below any person including myself. The team know our policies for all the formal stuff so when it is required to 'pull rank', we can have an effective grown-up conversation. To facilitate this, our management team have an open-door policy on the office, and given we operate a twenty-four seven service, if our team is on shift, our management team is on shift for emergency situations. Then, in those moments when something urgent does occur, we will be there either on the other end of the phone supporting the employee navigating the situation or physically getting to the site in person.

Supporting this practice is listening. Really listening … ensuring our tribe of amazing employees feel empowered to speak up, be heard and have what they've said be valued. For example, if an employee tells me they cannot work tomorrow, that is non-negotiable to me, and our team know that. This approach has allowed me to surround myself with amazing humans that support me, hear me, see me and make me want to be a better human simply because I treat them with the same equal respect.

We also celebrate the good stuff! If our employees are celebrating a birth, death, marriage, cultural festivals, graduation, divorce, first home, final exam, graduation, a community cause or achievement and we know about it … we celebrate! If it is important to our employee, it is important to us. We celebrate in a variety of ways, sometimes it's general gift cards, other times it could be something super personal. If our team members work on their birthdays, you can bet we will shower them with birthday love. Sharing in these milestones and achievements is just a small way we choose to recognise and support our tribe and show our appreciation. You are only ever as good as your team, and I am so grateful I have a phenomenal one!

UNSOLICITED ADVICE

For what it's worth … stop being your own worst enemy and remember this:

- Take control of your own narrative.
- Uncomfortable is where growth begins.
- Compassion is balance and flexibility.
- Perspective allows you to seek the silver linings.
- Your tribe are your people.

Lastly, as a wise woman once told me …

'Treat others how you wish to be treated.' – My mum

NATASHIA TELFER

Natashia is a Canberra-based mum, wife, sister, daughter, friend and businesswoman. She also considers herself a survivor, juggler and perpetual ball-dropper, chaos coordinator and silver lining seeker.

Natashia Telfer has worked within the health care sector for eighteen years in a variety of roles including aged care, disability, acquired brain injury, and now co-founder and director of National Community Care in Canberra. Natashia's compassion and driving force within the industry begun when she was faced with adversity at the age of eighteen when she was diagnosed with stage 4B cancer. Despite the odds, Natashia rose above it, pivoting the trajectory of her life and her purpose.

Today, Natashia is committed to ensuring her team provide the benchmark service to be rivalled with, believing the current standard is not good enough. Natashia believes every human deserves the right to access quality care in a way that meets their needs. National Community Care advocate and fight the fight for those most vulnerable, those that go unheard, for all the round pegs, the too-hard baskets, the forgotten ones. Natashia is not afraid of standing up and speaking out against unjust causes. She is a disruptor, fighting for systemic change endeavouring to improve the system to benefit those most vulnerable.

Natashia has been recognised for her committed efforts by many government bodies including NDIS, ACT Health, the Governor General, ADACAS, the Aged Care Practitioner Office, and the Human Rights Commissioner by simply advocating for those unheard. Natashia has been recognised in the Local Business Awards, the rubik3 CWB Businesswoman of the Year and Social Impact Businesswomen of the Year, the Women in Business Telstra Awards, AusMumprener of the

Year finalist, Health and Wellbeing Award, Business Excellence Award and B2B Service Business Award.

These efforts and drive of Natashia's have led her to a handful of side hustles including most recently 'Kindness and Courage' where she endeavours to inspire people to look after their mental health, find purpose and be their best selves through her podcast, upcoming solo book and K&C tribe. During the height of the COVID-19 lock-downs, Natashia pivoted her Kindness & Courage business and instead of launching subscription boxes, she repurposed the boxes and sent out two hundred sunshine boxes free to those needing some sunshine. This selfless act recently attracted attention and she was recognised by Nine Network's *Today* show for her acts of kindness. She is a force to be reckoned with and in her words, she is 'just getting started'.

Website: nationalcommunitycare.com.au
kindnessandcourage.com.au

THE COURAGE & CONFIDENCE TO CHANGE YOUR LIFE

Peace Mitchell

When my sister Katy and I first started our business, I believed that we had to work long hours and we had to be 'busy' to be successful. I believed the harder we worked, the more successful our business would be.

I thought that good customer service meant replying to emails and social media messages instantly, even if they came through at ten o'clock at night or on weekends. I believed that we had to be constantly checking and updating our social media.

The signs of burnout came quickly in that first year of business.

My house was so messy that I rarely had friends over because I didn't have time to clean up.

I often worked all weekend while my husband took the kids to the beach or even camping overnight without me. My marriage was okay, but my husband was cranky and in a bad mood all the time. I was tired too and resented having to do all this work plus keep up with all the housework on my own. It didn't seem fair.

I'd put on weight because I just didn't have time to think about eating healthily or preparing healthy food and certainly didn't have time to exercise. I felt bad about myself, and I ate whole blocks of chocolate to try to cheer myself up. I would get debilitating migraines and panic attacks.

The business was going okay but we certainly weren't seeing any amazing results for all this hard work we were putting in. No-one was thanking us for missing time with our families and spending all our weekends and every night working such long hours. And my kids complained that I was always on the computer.

I started resenting the business and questioning what the point of it was. I'd lost sight of why I'd started, and it felt like the harder I worked, the more resentful I became, and the more resentful I became, the more customers stopped coming as they picked up on my energy. I was working harder but achieving less. It was devastating, it didn't make sense and I didn't know what to do.

Things finally got so bad after missing yet another special family event I'd never get back that I knew things had to change.

I knew in my heart that work would always be there but that life wouldn't. I also knew that if things were going to change it was up to me to make the changes. It was up to me to prioritise my life and my family and to stop letting my business run me into the ground and take me away from my family.

I wanted to blame the business, but I realised that I had the power to change my life and no-one else could do it for me. I realised that owning your own business should give you the freedom to create the life you want, not make you into a slave to your work. I realised that I had the choice to make my business work for me the way I wanted it to work, instead of the other way around.

I also realised that if I didn't start controlling the business, the business would keep controlling me.

When I look back now, I see that the business was taking me away from my children, my husband, my friends and my physical and mental health. It was like a toxic relationship, one that I kept going back to but didn't know how to escape from.

I didn't want to let my business do this to me anymore.

I knew I had to change. I knew I couldn't keep doing this. And so I got clear on what I did want.

I wanted my business to be my friend and support the life that I was dreaming of.

I wanted my business to help me be:

- A loving mother.
- A healthier person.
- A happier wife.
- A better friend.

I realised it wasn't just about the money.

I realised that all the money in the world wasn't worth losing your health, your marriage or your relationships with your friends and family. I wanted things to be different.

I'd always had vision boards, but I knew it was time to create a new one, one where I fulfilled my personal goals and not just my business goals. On my new vision board, we took family holidays together, I lost weight, became healthy and wore new clothes, I had a happy husband and spent time with my children helping them to focus on their goals, my house was organised and I had fun with friends.

I kept working on the business, but I also stayed focused on my personal goals. They were hard habits to break.

Eating well took planning and quite a few months of adjustment. I was fortunate to have my sister as my accountability buddy. Making myself go to the gym was really hard in the beginning too, but I always felt proud of myself after I'd been. After twelve months of going to the gym, people didn't recognise me because I looked so good.

The changes in my marriage, though, were almost immediate. I couldn't believe what a difference it made to switch off the computer and just spend time with my husband after the kids had gone to bed. So simple, yet so profound. He just wanted to spend time with me.

My kids were happier too and started doing better at school.

I'll be honest, my life isn't perfect, sometimes there are still dishes in the sink and washing to fold and sometimes I do have to work a little on a weekend. But I always remind myself of how I want my life to look and the person I want to be.

You can change your life too.

Here are some of the secrets to how my sister and I changed our lives, from one of chaos, resentment and depression to one of order, fulfilment and happiness.

FIND CLARITY

Get clear on your personal and business goals. Think about what kind of life you want to live – you and only you can decide how it will be! Do you want to work a four-day week and have three days off every weekend? Do you want to work just one hour a day? Do you want to work mornings and have the rest of the day off? Do you want to sleep in and have free time during the day and only work at night? These are all CHOICES you can make. The concept of a nine to five workday, five days a week is not a rule that entrepreneurs have to stick to. You can work more or less, it's all up to you. But I've learnt that you have to choose, and you have to be in control, otherwise the business will control you.

We decided we wanted to work school hours, finish at three and not work at night or on weekends and only an hour or two each morning on school holidays. I then had a baby and cut my working time back even further. Taking twelve full weeks off in the time before and after she was born and then returning to work just one hour a day. It's all possible. I discovered that I could work exactly as much or as little as I wanted to and the business would still be there. It's all about planning, prioritising and structuring your business to support your goals.

BUSINESS EDIT

My business was controlling my life and I had to take a step back and look at why there was always so much to do! We realised that we had taken on too much. We had lots of side projects and things happening which were time consuming yet didn't produce a lot of money, traffic or results. We held onto things that we should have let go of and we were easily distracted by 'bright shiny objects' or projects which we thought would be fun, without really analysing whether they would be profitable or beneficial to our business goals. It took us a long time to really see this clearly but we've learnt that more is not always better.

We found that the key is to really think about the return on investment:

1. Identify what is the most important thing in your business and make it your priority.
2. Delegate, automate, scale back, shelve or eliminate everything else.

Identifying the priority was easy but we found delegating, scaling back, cutting and shelving really hard. We agonised over this for a long time, even though we knew deep down we had to do it. I'm not sure why we held on to these things for so long and I think perhaps fear was a part of it. Fear of letting go of something that we should keep. Making the wrong decision. Fear that someone else wouldn't look after our business the same way we would. But I knew in the end that we couldn't keep doing everything the way we were. Each time we let something go I felt better, happier, lighter. And over time I began to feel free again.

Thinking about the eighty-twenty rule really helped. When we looked at the return on investment – whether that's time, energy or cost – we found some activities were so time consuming but didn't bring in the results we wanted. For example, we were spending a lot of time, money and energy on having a physical presence at big in-person expos around Australia but the results were poor, we would only get a few hundred people sign up to our newsletter and then most would unsubscribe within a few months because they weren't the right audience for us in the first place. Whereas online activities would result in a lot more targeted subscribers who would stay subscribed long-term, become paying customers and cost a lot less in terms of time, money and effort. Taking the time to really assess this across all aspects of our business was a game changer.

ASK FOR HELP

No-one expects you to do everything by yourself, so why should you expect it of yourself? Finding the right people to work with in your business can take time, but it's worth it.

The zone of genius is that special thing you can do easily and effortlessly, it's your gift to the world. You know that you're working in your zone of genius when you're in a state of flow, where time passes without you realising. It's when you're working on something, and you feel content, happy and fulfilled to be doing something that you love.

Sadly, very few of us get to work in our zone of genius because we're weighed down by all the other mundane tasks that consume our time. Most people end up wasting time in their zone of competence – or worse, their zone of mediocrity – with their time overrun by dull admin tasks that they don't even enjoy but are reluctant to delegate to someone else.

Outsourcing work is the best way to grow your business. Delegating essential but time-consuming tasks to a virtual assistant or team member allows you to focus on the big picture goals instead of getting tied up in the trivial day-to-day tasks. It can also create consistency, if you organise it to be this way with dedicated systems.

It can be hard to ask for help or favours from family and friends but this is important too. Children as young as three and four can start helping out by packing up toys and I've found that the school mums are often happy to have a child over to occupy their own child once or twice a week. Who do you have around you who can help support you?

BATCH AND AUTOMATE

For the tasks that you do need to complete yourself, batching is an excellent strategy to employ. Batching involves working on similar jobs together rather than doing them sporadically throughout the day or the week. A great example is batching your emails, if you have a number of emails coming through about the same thing or project, create a label in your inbox and mark them with this, then create a standard reply that you can copy and paste then tailor individually so that you can quickly and easily reply to all of them at the same time rather than as each one comes through.

Similarly, scheduling allows you to batch activities such as blog posts or social media. By scheduling content you can plan and organise all of your social media updates for the week instead of spending time on this each day. It's a great time-saver as social media can be both distracting and a drain on time and productivity.

Automating is a huge time-saver too. Identify things in your business that can be automated to happen without you thinking about them. Setting up automated systems and processes can take time and energy initially but will save you hours in the long run.

SET BOUNDARIES

The one thing that made the biggest difference for me was setting boundaries around my time. Working when the children were at school and then switching off when they were home has helped me balance my time so much better. When I know that I only have a certain amount of time, I'm more likely to be focused and productive while I can and tick off as many goals as possible within that time. When you have all day to do something, it's easy for tasks to take all day. Being present for your family when they need you is important for you and for them and will help everything else in your life flow so much better.

Nurturing your relationships can only happen if you make time for them. Make time for a date night once a month. Spend time with your children one-on-one doing activities you both love. Have fun experiencing new things as a family on the weekends. It's so easy to get stuck in a rut so shake things up if you're experiencing this and have fun with your time.

MAKE TIME FOR YOURSELF

When you feel better, your business does better. People can tell. It's contagious and they want to be around you. The best thing I ever did for my business was joining the gym and becoming fit and healthy. It seems crazy that I spent less time working on the business and more time working on myself and yet the business benefitted! A morning workout gives me clarity, energy and focus. I use the time to reflect on the goals ahead and set my intention for the day. A morning workout also means you're more likely to eat well during the rest of the day, and when these two things become a habit your whole life, health and outlook changes.

Looking after yourself is also about finding time to do things that you enjoy. Reading a book, having a cup of tea, watching a TV show you like, art, cooking, crafts, catching up with friends for a coffee are all little things you can do to nourish your wellbeing. Something small every day just for you is important. If you need to organise someone to mind your kids so you can do this occasionally then ask for help. If you're not happy and well, how can you look after your family?

When I look back to those early days in our business and how hard we found it to get our business off the ground, I feel sad that we had to go through that struggle and that we didn't have the support or guidance to know how to manage our time and our business the right way. I'm so grateful that we took the time to look at where we could make changes and had the courage to implement and action those changes.

Although my life isn't always perfect and there are times when I do need to work more, it's not every day and I'm in control of when I do work and when I don't. I'm now happier, healthier and have a better marriage than ever before! Our business is successful, fulfilling, rewarding and profitable and I have more time to spend with my family too.

Changing your life is possible. It starts with you taking that first step to recognise what you want your life to be like and then having the courage and the confidence to make it so.

PEACE MITCHEL

Peace Mitchell is an investor, author, international keynote speaker, CEO and co-founder of The Women's Business School, AusMumpreneur and Women Changing The World Press and the Australian ambassador of Women in Tech.

Peace is passionate about supporting women to reach their full potential and create the life they want to live. She has helped thousands of women achieve their dream of running a successful and profitable business and believes that investing in women is the best way to change the world.

Peace Mitchell and her sister Katy Garner co-founded Aus-Mumpreneur in 2009 creating Australia's number one community for mothers in business and co-founded The Women's Business School in 2016 to provide entrepreneurial education for women globally.

Today, her commitment is stronger than ever to invest in the power of women to change the world.

'Through providing education, inspiration, guidance, connection and support for women, we are committed to providing access to education for women from all walks of life, all over the world. Our programs have been designed to provide connection with experienced women in business from a range of industries and backgrounds.'

We are proud to be creating better opportunities for entrepreneurial education for women globally through:

ADVOCACY

Passionate about supporting women, Peace has worked in advocacy with all levels of government to create change. Peace has been instrumental in being a voice for women by changing local government legislation to create more inclusive town planning at a local level, calling for a national conversation on women entrepreneurs at a federal level and partnering with the Queensland State Government to provide $1 million in grants for small business owners at state level.

EDUCATION

Investing in women is the most powerful way to change the world and it's this philosophy which has driven Peace's vision to create a global business school for women. In just three years, The Women's Business School has seen four hundred women graduate, created partnerships with global brands including World Pulse, Emerging Women and Tererai Trent International and school alumni have won awards, received investor funding, been invited to speak internationally and taken their brands to global markets.

ACTIVISM

In working with thousands of Australian women entrepreneurs over the past twelve years, Peace has discovered a surprising trend. Women aren't starting businesses to make money – they're starting businesses to create change. Today, women-led businesses are far more likely to be focused on helping people, creating a more sustainable environment and generally making the world a better place in their own unique, beautiful and creative way. What if we could inspire people everywhere to change the world in a small way? This was the inspiration for *Women Will Change the World TV* – a weekly Facebook Live show focused on inspiring purpose, vision and everyday activism featuring women changing the world through entrepreneurialism, conscious living, advocacy and innovation.

AMPLIFYING

We believe that providing a platform for women's voices is so important, women have the power to change the world but we must work together to help bring these voices to the world and let their message be heard. We do this through our books, podcasts, website features and in-person events.

INVESTING

We believe investing in women is the most powerful way to change the world and our future vision includes creating opportunities for women to invest financially in each others' businesses through becoming shareholders.

Women hold the key to unlock the solutions to all of the problems the world is facing and it's up to all of us to come together to lift women up!

Website: thewomensbusinessschool.com

wcwpress.com

ausmumpreneur.com

CHASING DREAMS

Samantha Richards

Having lived in seven countries – Malta, Iran, UK, Sudan, Nigeria, Cyprus and now Australia – my life has been pretty extraordinary on every level.

As a child, I was curious about everything. Some of my dreams included becoming an astronaut, fighter pilot, marine biologist, archaeologist, doctor, vet, police officer, private investigator, professional athlete, writer and actress. My list was endless and utterly diverse. However, by the time I was fourteen, my life experiences had torn those dreams apart.

My life had become one of displacement and violence. Not only did I lose the ability to chase my dreams, but I also pushed them away, believing I had no right to have goals.

I went from a life full of excitement and curiosity to one where I simply existed in the world. I allowed my primal instincts to take over in order to survive. As time went on, I developed suicidal ideologies (I just wanted the pain to go away) but never dared to follow through. I stopped living my life to the full because I'd allowed other people to take from me what was rightfully mine.

Now, I'm glad my ideas of self-harm never amounted to anything, though I emotionally and psychologically beat myself up (due to my unhealthy inner dialogue), which is also a form of self-harm. I now see my life as one where my experiences allow me to help educate others in developing a healthy voice.

Even though many things have happened to me over my lifetime, one event stands out, and it's one that's stopped me from throwing my hands in the air and yelling, 'That's it, I give up!'

Before I tell the story, I want to tell you a little more about what has happened in my life recently that's challenged my dream-chasing again.

I'm a mother of two and had been with my partner for twenty-three years. In October 2021, my husband became my ex-husband (I call him my 'was-band', which sounds nicer on the ear than 'ex').

The decision left me feeling like a teenager starting all over again. Only this time, I had multiple responsibilities as a single mother and no direct family members around me (aside from my two children) in a country that wasn't my original home. I had never felt more alone, as I was kicked to the curb by the person for whom I'd left everything behind.

Ten months after my father passed away and two days before my birthday in 2016, my husband told me that he didn't find me sexually attractive anymore because I had put on weight (I'd quit smoking and gained a total of 26kg). I felt utterly fat-shamed by the one person who was supposed to love me for who I was. I moved out of the marital bed and slept on the couch for five years.

Still, this new blow made me feel humiliated, as I had already looked for a solution to my weight gain because I felt uncomfortable anyway. I kept trying to lose weight, eventually plateauing in my efforts. Finally, I asked my husband to help me by cooking the family meals so I could go on a strict diet. He took up the gauntlet, and it took me two years to lose it all.

I successfully removed the weight gain 'objection'. However, it transpired that something far more profound was going on with my partner. We had an argument where I told him I couldn't be in a loveless relationship. He said he'd get help, and although he went to the doctor, he didn't fully follow through. Instead, he admitted he had developed a deep resentment towards me during a conversation. His feelings of resentment were the nail in the coffin for our troubled relationship. He resented the fact that I hadn't cooked for two years, and his resentment prevented him from crossing the intimacy barrier his mind had created.

I will accept that I threatened to leave him many times over the years, but I never went. When a woman threatens but doesn't leave, it's a cry for help. It's a plea for the other person to not only listen but to action too. I never felt heard.

All I have ever wanted was for him to be kind and loving towards me, not just when it suited him. I wanted our relationship to work, and I tried, and I guess in his mind, he did too. I wanted him to seek help, which he'd sporadically get when pushed, then he'd stop. Part of me feels he simply hoped our issues would go away.

I wanted him to get the same help I had sought, so he could understand more fully why my weight gain repulsed him. After all, I was still the same person he had married all those years ago, and at the time, I had given up smoking (not anymore), a habit he hated.

I had put on weight, and although I had difficulty shifting it, excess weight could be lost. However, words and how we're made to feel can never be forgotten.

At fifty-three, it's daunting to be single again. However, some of my life experiences keep reminding me of my strengths. There's always something positive to be gained when the initial negatives pass.

Reflection truly is a beautiful thing!

Reflecting back over my time line, I stopped at an experience when

I was twenty years old when I worked for the British High Commission in Lagos, Nigeria, as a personal assistant to the first secretary of the commercial and economic department.

Aside from my usual duties as an assistant, I also acted as his host at parties when the first secretary's wife couldn't attend. My favourite part of the job was when we investigated cases of alleged fraud.

Whenever a Nigerian company contacted one in Britain, we would receive a telex asking if they were legitimate. We would go and verify the claims. My boss would do all the talking, and I would sit and listen intently, watching for body language signals and telltale signs of deception in their tone of voice.

I absolutely loved my job. I felt like a private investigator, only I didn't have to observe from afar – seriously, it was awesome!

In my private time, I would hang out at Tarkwa Bay (the beach) with my friends, where we would ride in speedboats, swim, waterski and have a few drinks. We would go to the nightclubs and dance the night away. One of my male friends taught me how to play blackjack at the casino, playing with house money. What I won I could keep, but I had to give back the initial sum they gave me. What a life it was!

Then one day, the unthinkable happened.

I was in a diplomatic car on my way home. We were pulled over by men in uniform. This wasn't uncommon, as we were regularly pulled over. Usually, after handing over some money ('I dash you' means 'I'll give you money'), we would leave. This time, the man's body language signalling for us to stop seemed off; his hand moved to the gun on his hip. *Oh shit,* I thought.

I put my hand on my driver's shoulder and muttered, 'Do nothing, I've got this.'

We pulled to a stop, and I opened my window. The uniformed man yanked my door open, reached in with his weaponed hand and held his gun to my head. He commanded, 'Come down from de car!'

When I'd first arrived in Lagos, I was told that if I was ever stopped and told to get out of the car, I was to stay where I was; I didn't move.

Something told me that if I did, the man was going to rape and kill me – my life flashed before my eyes. With everything to lose and everything to gain, I kept my voice as even as I could and bravely said, 'No!' I pushed the gun away.

The man grabbed a fistful of my hair and put the gun back to my head, and shouted, 'Come down from de car!' I felt his spittle splash in my eyes.

This time, I turned my head and looked into his eyes. Defiantly, I answered, 'No!'

The man really lost his temper, and through gritted teeth, he snarled. He began pulling me from the car by my hair. 'Come down from de car, or I shoot you in de head!'

Those horrifying few moments seemed like an eternity to me. My driver's knuckles paled as he gripped the steering wheel. I touched his shoulder again and squeezed. I couldn't let him intervene. If he did, he would have been executed on the spot – I couldn't let him die for me. As crazy as this sounds, I had a much better chance of survival because I was white. My driver didn't move, but I could feel his panicked energy fill the car.

My own panic rose to the surface. I could feel my heart pounding in my chest and the colour drain from my face. I knew my time was running out. Still, I sat in my seat and faced my tormentor.

To this day, I'm profoundly grateful for my ability to read human behaviour so well. When I looked into his eyes, I saw fear. Fear for his own mortality if he followed through and got caught because justice would have been served. Murdering a white woman would not have gone unnoticed.

He decided it was worth the risk, but the fear that I saw in his eyes as I defied him gave me the courage to do what I did next.

I firmly grabbed the wrist that held my hair, and as calmly as my beating heart and addled mind would allow, I decided to become a chameleon. I'm good at accents, pidgin English being one of my strongest.

I spoke to him using the same accent he used with me. By doing this, I was unconsciously letting him know that I had lived in Lagos for a long time. That I wasn't some random tourist.

I told the sweating face pressed so close to mine, 'If you shoot me, you cause a political incident. Go look for de number plate and tell me, do you want to be hunted down like a dog by de British government?' I saw his eyes widen slightly; I had hit home!

As a locally engaged employee of the British High Commission, I had no diplomatic immunity. Still, when your life hangs in the balance, you're willing to say and do anything to save yourself and anyone else that might be in danger too.

The fact that I was in a diplomatic car saved my life. It was a gamble that I'd chosen to take. A risky one, but what else was I to do? I was not going to comply and get out of the car. Even though I had some martial arts training in Shotokan and judo, I knew I wasn't proficient enough to disarm him and then take on the other two men standing by his side.

I made a split-second decision that if my ruse didn't work, I was going to go down fighting, and I would try to take one down with me.

The man released me and went to look at the number plate. The fear in his eyes heightened as he re-evaluated his position of what may happen if he continued with his demands. He came to a decision, backed away from the car and gestured for us to pass.

It was a fortunate escape; others had not been so lucky. A Nigerian girlfriend of mine told me that she'd been shot in the arm when the same thing happened to her.

Was this brave or stupid of me? I don't know, but I can tell you this: I was absolutely terrified throughout the whole ordeal. Time slowed down as I thought for ways to survive a gun attack. Everything in my life flashed before my eyes – my family, childhood and dreams. The amount of processing that must have been going on in my head at the time now feels incredible.

This scrape with my own mortality highlighted that our primal instinct of survival is unimaginable when faced with situations over which we feel we have no control. It can help us to see things we might never usually notice.

Though the man had the balance of power in his favour in that terrifying altercation, he was working from a self-serving level. Having grown up in so many countries, I've had the advantage of observing behaviour patterns in my fellow human beings. The man didn't realise that I had psychologically entered his brain (even when terrified) and made him doubt his own survival if I was harmed.

In that particular case, it became a battle of the survival of the fittest. This might sound like a brag, and I don't mean it to be, but I don't know how to express it any other way, other than a realisation that I was the stronger of the two. Not physically, but psychologically. I didn't use fists, weapons or force to survive a possible rape and murder. I used words and the power of suggestion to plant seeds of doubt into a person I believed to be an opportunist.

Was someone watching over me that day? I like to think so. Sometimes I wonder if they watch over me and chat amongst themselves. 'Oh crap, here we go again. All hands on deck, she's got herself into another sticky situation!' If I do have guardian angels, they've certainly had their work cut out over my lifetime in keeping me alive.

We hear so many stories daily where people take advantage of those they believe to be weaker than them. My account isn't one of the weaknesses of a woman incapable of fighting her way out of situations. My story highlights the ability to intellectually negotiate a way out of a potentially fatal position by appealing to a person's sense of self-preservation.

By staying as calm as I could, I was able to reason clearly and look for a way out. I managed to maintain a rationale that saved my life and the life of my driver.

I learned that day (though it took me years to work out) that good communication and observational abilities should be taught more in schools. If we give our children the tools to stay calm and think clearly when young, they're more likely to approach most situations without their egos taking centrestage.

When we learn to communicate well, we can actively modulate our tone to not antagonise. We can observe body language to see what's really being said, and we can speak in a way that'll allow us to live our lives with some modicum of harmony.

I was never taught how to communicate well as a child – my learning came from the hard knocks of life. That said, I do wish I'd learned how in school, but they didn't offer anything like that when I was a kid.

In that terrifying event, my street smarts offered me an advantage. However, I'd love to see that advantage provided to every person.

All my life experiences have offered me something. Would I change them? Maybe some, but not this one. This one showed me I have what it takes to survive. It showed me a side of myself I never knew existed, and I quite like that side.

We are meant to live life, and dreams should be chased unashamedly. I don't take anything for granted and see my gift of life – a life that might have been cut short – to be one that should be celebrated!

SAMANTHA RICHARDS

Samantha Richards is Australia's top public speaking coach (*Yahoo! Finance*), a TEDx speaker, and is the founder of Building Voices Public Speaking, a communication coaching business that works with children to develop lifelong skills as confident communicators.

Early in her career as a communication coach, Samantha realised that a social need exists for children to develop communication skills not fully learned during their formative years at school (outside of debate and drama). She discovered a practical demand in an area that should better serve our children's needs. The need resulted in the development of the junior public speaking program, where she teaches children confident communication, builds self-esteem, encourages positive leadership and develops essential and comprehensive life skills.

Samantha recently launched Building Voices Communication for adults who want to take their business to the next level. This platform helps people share their untold stories and to step into their power to be seen, which will enable them to be positioned as an authority in their field.

It is because of the adversity Samantha has had to overcome that she found the courage to share her experiences with others, to help them find their voice, create their victories and make them masters of their destinies.

Samantha services the emotional, mental and physical needs of children and adults by developing growth, confidence, mental health and wellbeing through teaching good communication techniques. By offering skills that have a far-reaching impact on both the personal and business lives of her clients, they can develop healthily in every way.

Samantha has helped split families communicate more effectively, which has positively impacted the children. She has helped children learn to negotiate rather than fight with their parents, bringing about a more peaceful family atmosphere. She has consistently produced strong school leaders through her coaching programs.

For adults, Samantha has found that when they realise how different communication styles will produce different results, they have been able to adapt their communication style accordingly to generate their desired outcome, both at home and at work.

Website: buildingvoicescommunication.com (adults)
buildingvoices.com.au (kids)
Email: samantha_richards@buildingvoices.com.au
Phone: +61 409 110169

THE COURAGE TO LEAP

Business lessons I didn't realise my
mother taught me

Sandy Davies

Without being consciously aware until recently, I action the business lessons I learned from my mother every single day.

I champion her wins. I rave about her inspiration and the difference she made to other women, but not until her passing did I become completely aware of how much I, too, absorbed from her example.

My mother passed away shortly before I re-emerged from semiretirement to start one last business, a business of the heart to help other women. Even though I've been a businesswoman all my life, this final hurrah provides the platform that would have meant the most to my mother.

In this most meaningful of all my endeavours, I felt orphaned without my biggest cheerleader to listen to my woes, share her knowledge, provide guidance and celebrate the wins. But as the business has grown, I feel my mother's beautiful lingering presence gently hovering over my shoulder like a ray of sunshine at every tough corner. And with that presence is the realisation that long before she departed she had indeed taught me all the business lessons I'll ever need to know.

My mother instilled in me the courage to leap. Because of her, I try not to take things personally, I know that attitude is everything, I've learned to be true to myself, I always feed my people, and most importantly, I never lose the courage to leap. Nor should you. You are never too old and it is never too late. Whatever it is you dream of doing, you have totally got this. If any doubt remains, my wish for you is that it shrinks to dust by the end of this chapter.

DON'T TAKE IT PERSONALLY, KEEP MOVING FORWARD

At the age of fifty, my post-World War II mother found herself entering the world of mainstream employment for the first time. She didn't have a choice. Economic circumstance forced her into a sink or swim moment. She swam. Often against the current. Often facing rejection. Often with the expectation of failure simply because she was a woman in a man's game. But she swam nonetheless. She became a glass ceiling breaker. She went on to mentor other women in her male-dominated industry. I idolised her like a real-life Violet from the movie *9 to 5*.

To this day I still think of my mother killin' it in the 1980s whenever I hear Dolly Parton's theme song to that movie. Never forget in those moments of struggle which accompany every business, your tide will turn.

One of my close teen friends in high school became a friend and colleague of my mother in adulthood. During our friend's own rise to the top, she recalls incorporating the following business tips from my mother:

1. Never forget to smile. Your radiance matters.
2. Being a woman has nothing to do with whether or not you can do a job.
3. Be genuine with people and truly help them through what you do.
4. Be kind to everyone, even if they are not nice to you. You never know when they might end up needing your services again.

5. Don't give up. Don't get discouraged easily. Don't take it personally. You might face ninety-nine rejections, but the hundredth could be the one.

Sometimes that last one, *don't take it personally,* can be the hardest lesson of all, which is why I want to share this rather embarrassing moment with you:

'Waaaaaaaaaaaaaaa! I want my mommy!' I felt like a six-year-old.

Yes, those are the words this grown-arse fifty-something woman cried into the arms of her husband after a defeating business blow.

I had been slated to speak at our little sugarcane town's women's health expo until an urban doctor expressed interest in participating. I got dropped like a hot potato rather than keeping us both on the rostrum. It was the climax in a week of rejections. A high-profile wellness hamper business I'd been negotiating with knocked me back at the zero hour because my brand was 'not yet familiar enough and would prevent sales'. A podcaster cancelled our chat because of my age stating she 'preferred femtrepreneurs at the start of their journey not the end'. The snub by the local ladies after a week of blows tipped me over the edge.

Luckily my husband didn't choose that moment to question whether my tears were real or menopausal, he simply held me in his arms, wiped away my tears and assured me it would all get better the same way we comforted our daughters when they were little. I missed my beautiful mom so much in that overwhelming moment of defeat.

Despite wanting my mother back here on earth more than anything, I realised, just like the first time the training wheels come off and we ride our big-girl bike all on our own, we do find our balance and we do possess everything we need for success inside us. In that moment of tears when you do take it personally, rest assured, the moment will pass.

Did I mention that I felt like I was six years old? That's because I was six the time I skated a bit too far away from home. I stacked it in a spectacular crash that would leave this digitally connected era in utter awe if body cameras had been a thing in the 1970s. I would've gone viral for sure!

I sat there bloodied and bruised on the ground, wailing for my mother. And then it hit me: being confident enough to rollerskate too far meant, whether I wanted the comfort of my mother or not, I skated myself into a position where I was the only one who could take care of me.

Still whimpering, I picked myself up, gathered what pride I had left and determinedly stood up to skate back home for bandaids. As I turned around, I saw my mother running up the street, arms open wide ready to brush my tears away and make everything all better. Of course, I leapt – skates and all – into those welcoming arms of comfort. But the lesson had already been learned in the moment of rising up on my own.

We all fall down, we all have moments of rejection, we all cry, but we determine our success in the moment of getting up.

'Everyone has to deal with tough times. A gold medal doesn't make you immune to that. A skater is used to falling down and getting up again.'
– Dorothy Hamill, 1976 Olympic Champion

When you, too, find yourself wailing, force yourself to get a solid sleep. After a good night's sleep, tomorrow is always brighter. Keep moving forward. Get up; you've got this.

ATTITUDE IS EVERYTHING

Life will throw you curve balls. You will have days when you question why you ever went into business. But the mindset you choose will determine your direction and how you navigate those challenging moments.

Years ago, someone had disappointed me or let me down. I can no longer recall the teenage drama that occurred but I am thankful it led to my mother posting this note on the bathroom mirror before I got up the next morning. Her message has resonated within my soul ever since:

'The important and decisive factor in life is not what happens to us; but the attitude we take toward what happens.'
– Leona Skelton, Sandy's Mother

We cannot control the behaviour of others, but we can control our attitude and how we react. I decided a long, long time ago that letting others steal my joy gave them too much power.

I grew up in the wheat belt of the American Midwest. Rural counties had driving laws that allowed kids as young as fourteen to get their driving licence. The purpose was to enable farm kids to drive wheat trucks to the elevators during harvest, but it also meant that all us country kids got to legally drive from a very young age, even if we could only barely see over the steering wheel. It was awesome! It equated driving with freedom, especially on the wide-open highways of the Great Plains.

Whenever my mother needed a driver, I was her gal. I spent many of my teen years driving those long highways to attend motivational seminars with my mother as she built her career. Early on, I handwrote a message from one of those seminars and taped it where I would see it as a daily reminder. I can't remember if it was Zig Ziglar, Louise Hay, Wayne Dyer, Tony Campolo or Steven Covey who pointed their finger at the little girl in the front row at the Cosmopshere Convention Centre in Hutchinson, Kansas, and said, 'If you let someone else ruin your day, they've won,' but to this day, they are totally right.

Like my mama said, your radiance matters. Stay focused on that joy that emanates from within rather than letting others spoil your day. There's something about lifting the corners of your lips that connects to the receptors in your brain to reset your attitude to get you back on track to get through the rest of the day.

'Joy does not simply happen to us. We have to choose joy and keep choosing it every day.' – Henri JM Nouwen

BE TRUE TO YOURSELF

There were so many people in my mother's industry who were driven by greed and focused only on sales, sales, sales rather than the needs of their clients. Even in times where she wasn't sure if she would be able to pay our bills at the end of the month, she always put the genuine needs of her clients first.

Ethics are everything. I'm grateful to my mother for teaching me that, in business, if you look after the people your business serves with a genuine heart, you can trust that the money will follow. Doing right by your customers ensures you sleep soundly at night. It helps your business grow in a way that you can be proud of with no regrets.

I learned many years ago that whenever someone drops 'business is business' into the conversation, the next recommended action will be something dodgy or unethical. If it is not acceptable within your inner circle in your personal life, don't let it be acceptable in your business. Extricate yourself whenever you hear that phrase.

In hindsight, I do think I tiptoed far too often in those early years in business. I would find myself entangled with suppliers longer than I should for the sake of being polite. Value who you invest in and don't waste time keeping the wrong people in your network. As soon as it doesn't feel right, cast aside worrying about whether removing yourself is polite or not. Whether it is your solicitor, financial advisor, accountant, project manager or an external service provider, don't tread water.

Move your business away from those who don't align with your values. Good people gravitate to one another and you will find your trusted tribe. I would have saved thousands of dollars and many nights of worry over the years if I had walked away in the very first instance whenever my gut gave me a nudge …

'Listen to the quiet of your inner voice, she will not lead you astray.'
— *Sandy Davies to Deborah Voll,* Calm the Chaos *Podcast*

Be true to yourself. At your core, you know your path. Shut off the outside noise and do what you know is right for you and for your business. You are your best advocate.

FEED YOUR PEOPLE

Through all my years in business, our competitors were regularly jealous of our amazing teams. I never realised our team cultivation was unusual until I semiretired and entered the workplace as an employee of others. It is such an impersonal and callous world out there. If you are lucky enough to be an entrepreneur and your business grows to need a team, throw out the playbook. If you follow the traditional rules of employment you will create an ordinary workplace like all the others achieving ordinary results. Do it your way.

For me, feeding everyone's strengths is essential. Create opportunities for team members to soar. Create a workplace where you can't wait to see your favourite team members reach the point where they are ready to strike out on their own to make their business dreams come true. Create a workplace where everyone is safe and valued for what they bring to the table.

Our biggest secret was simple: love your team like family. Yet another trait I subconsciously garnered from my mother. I am thankful I never realised treating people like family within the workplace was out of the ordinary until we had semiretired. My jaw still drops to the floor when I hear respected company owners drop mean-spirited, impersonal comments about their personnel. Regardless of wealth, if they've failed as a human being and being a decent employer, I lose all respect.

Your team are not chattels. If your business is from the heart, love your team like family. When we moved north of the Tropic of Capricorn, over a dozen long-term team members visited to celebrate our new tropical life and contribute to building our home, largely because they became family.

Unfortunately, cultivating a strong family environment puts you in a position of trust where you have to make tough decisions. My biggest takeaway from all our years in business is to figure out your own way to be confident in letting the wrong people go without delay. The cohesiveness of your team depends on you finding the strength to be able to learn this difficult but crucial skill.

You will invariably pick the wrong person for the job on occasion. When it happens, you know. Sometimes you know before lunch the first day. Other times you realise six weeks in. Sometimes you can't see it initially, but your most trusted team members do. Whenever it happens, strike hard and fast. Pay the wrong choice out and move on. You maintain the respect of your team and you maintain an environment where everyone wants to bring their best to the table because there are no rotten apples. One bad team member has the potential to frustrate and bring everyone down. When that happens, the biggest loser is you and your business.

Creating your dream team is not solely about feeding team members' strengths; it is also about literally providing nourishment. Joy and aha moments that take your business to the next level often occur around a table of food, openness and laughter.

After my mother retired in America, we brought her out to be with us in Australia on an aged parent visa. Once a fortnight she would bring morning tea up to our team at our workshop. Everyone looked forward to it and important conversations that improved our business happened at that roundtable.

Once my mother knew someone's favourite food, it always appeared. Thankfully, I followed her lead. Some of my favourite dishes at barbecues today are favourite dishes of team members from thirty years ago. Priceless. Feed your people.

The value of food is about more than you feeding your team; sometimes you need to let them feed you. Be willing to change up the recipe through the ingredients new members bring to the team. The most unconventional relationships can be the most powerful for innovative moments that propel your business forward. Take Martha Stewart and Snoop Dogg.

'I want to be alongside this lady for the rest of my life. People can get along, people can work together, people can love each other, no matter where they come from or how they were brought up.'
— Snoop Dogg on his friendship with Martha Stewart

Watching Martha be open to adding Snoop Dogg's secret ingredient to fried chicken on their MTV show *Martha & Snoop's Potluck Dinner Party* was magic. Snoop blew Martha's mind and changed the way she prepped fried chicken forevermore. Always be open to being wowed by the magic others can bring to your business and your life.

THE COURAGE TO LEAP — YOU ARE NEVER TOO OLD, IT IS NEVER TOO LATE

As a small-town girl growing up in rural Kansas, I always yearned for something more. I was the first in my family to go to college straight after high school. Then I was awarded a fellowship to complete my master's degree overseas. Competing against thousands of other applicants for the fellowship, I wasn't sure if I would stand a chance or not when most recipients came from privileged backgrounds.

I couldn't believe it when I was selected; all my Christmases came at once. My mother was even prouder. Becoming an ambassador of goodwill as a Rotary Foundation scholar to complete my master's degree in Australia was a dream come true.

'All our dreams come true, if we have the courage to pursue them.'
– Walt Disney

Both my mother and I were so excited that we never expected the cacophony of dissent as the time for my departure neared. I was an adult in my mid-twenties fully capable of making decisions for myself, yet with the exception of the owner of the local car dealership, every other person in our small town scolded my mother with the exact same shaming words, 'How can you LET Sandy go to Australia?' The connotation conveyed the question would not have been asked had I been a son.

For decades after I did go to Australia, my mother would speak at motivational seminars. She would tell this story and end it with, 'How could I *NOT* let my daughter leap into the life she was destined for?'

I know myself well enough to know I would have leapt with or without her support, but I am thankful she had my back and 'let' me go. Years later, when our youngest daughter decided to go to the United Kingdom to work abroad, I thought times had changed until someone asked me, 'How can you let your daughter go to the UK?' There was that darned permission word again.

At this point I need to confess: I have a lifelong affliction. When people ask me questions that beggar belief, Medusa-esque snakes involuntarily sprout from my head. I'm sure that wasn't the first Medusa moment of my life, nor will it be my last, but I vividly remember the asker of that question watch my eyes fill with sparks and make a hasty exit just as the snakes emerged. At least when I had to wear the mama shoes, it was only one person, not an entire town. I am thankful that the gender equity message is finally sticking with this next generation.

Our daughter went. She soared. And now, when I expected to be finished soaring, I am again catching the uplift of that entrepreneurial breeze. Here I am, in my fifties, breaking down stereotypes around menopause and pushing past age barriers. Through the stories others share with me, I am discovering there are still far too many of us letting fear hold us back or postponing our dreams.

'Twenty years from now you will be more disappointed by the things you didn't do than by the ones you did. Throw off the bowlines, sail away from the safe harbour. Catch the trade winds in your sails. Explore. Dream. Discover.' – Apocryphal Mark Twain, most likely the words of Sarah Frances Brown

If you've been dreaming of something and questioning whether you are ready to take the risk or not, let me let you in on a little secret: you are ready. You have got this. You are never too old – or too young, for that matter. And it is most certainly never too late. Don't let fear hold you back. The worst that can happen is you fail. So what? Take in the lessons learned, pick yourself up, put your skates back on and try again.

The only thing worse than not taking the leap? Regret.

Leap!

SANDY DAVIES

Long before the creation of HappyPause Balm, Sandy Davies was born and raised in the American Midwest in the state of Kansas. Sandy immigrated to Australia to do her master's degree in social policy at the University of New South Wales in Sydney as a Rotary Fellow and Ambassador of Goodwill for Rotary International.

After graduate school, tourism beckoned. Sandy operated an adventure tourism business with her partner on World Heritage Listed Fraser Island for decades. Once their girls were grown, they sold their business and semiretired to the tropical idylls of Far North Queensland … or so they thought.

An allergic reaction to a treatment for intimate dryness during perimenopause launched Sandy out of semiretirement. She is now the Queensland-based formulator and founder of the award-winning HappyPause Balm. As a bit of a rebel who struggles taking 'no' for an answer, Sandy turned the lack of a simple, preservative-free natural solution for intimate dryness into her mission.

The creation of HappyPause is Sandy's 'yes'. The most recent research shows that almost 80% of women over forty will experience vulval vaginal dryness, yet because such issues were never spoken about in past generations, treatment options remain sparse and relatively unchanged for decades. A tiny pearl of HappyPause puts a spring back in your step. Dryness caused by peri/postmenopause, chemotherapy, endometriosis, type one diabetes, endurance training and other issues should never be a death knell to doing the active things we love, which is why creating HappyPause has brought Sandy so much joy in her second spring.

At every chapter of her life Sandy has thrived on giving back as a part of her ethos. Be it through Habitat for Humanity, Planned Parenthood, building projects in Guatemala, fundraising for Shed the Light Orphanage in Nepal, reading for The Royal Society for the Blind or contributing through Lifeline Australia, giving back has always mattered.

In this HappyPause era, Sandy's Pay It Forward Partner is The Period Project. The Period Project is an arm of the National Homeless Collective coordinated by 2021 Victorian Australian of the Year Donna Stolzenberg. To learn more about Donna's tireless work or make a donation to help eradicate period poverty visit nhcollective.org.au

When not packaging and processing orders and heightening menopause awareness, Sandy enjoys writing and spending time with her husband and their dog Karma on the isolated beaches of the tropics. Her book *The Power to Rise Above* about resilience and teenage bullying will be available in 2023.

Website: happypause.com.au
Instagram: happypause_menopause

HAVING THE CONFIDENCE TO PIVOT

Sarah Stoddart

We hear women talking about their desire to do something different and to forge their own destiny but so many decide not to take the leap of faith to pivot in a new direction. Unfortunately, it is often their own confidence that is holding them back.

If you're one of those women, it's time bring your dream to reality. In this chapter, I outline five key tips which you can follow to give yourself the confidence to pivot in a new direction.

FIVE STEPS TO HAVING THE CONFIDENCE TO PIVOT

1. WHAT'S THE WORST THAT CAN HAPPEN?

Contemplating any pivot in life can be daunting. You can find yourself going down rabbit holes of what-ifs and creating scenarios that may or may not come to fruition.

When I was contemplating starting my business, I was going around in circles in my head – conjuring up scenarios and filling myself with endless self-doubt. I had no self-belief and wasn't able to allow myself to recognise the opportunities that were in front of me. Sound familiar?

One Saturday afternoon, as the jacarandas bloomed in Brisbane, I found myself sitting on my friend's balcony in tears and very unsure of what step to take next in my career. Do I stick with what I know but which isn't going to work for me anymore, or do I take a leap of faith and make a change?

My friend had been in a similar situation to what I was in, and she had gone on to develop three very successful businesses. After the tears started to ease, we workshopped some of the key metrics of small business, including the minimum amount of money that I would have to make to feed my family and the basic set-up costs for the business. We were comfortable (my friend more than me!) that I could achieve those metrics. Sure, I wouldn't start out on the same salary that I was used to, but I'd be able to put food on the table, work the hours I wanted to work and still spend time with my family. And that's when my friend looked at me and asked, 'What's the worst that can happen?' It was my light-bulb moment. What *IS* the worst that can happen? The business doesn't work out and I get a job.

Immediately following that discussion, I decided to go for it. I went home and started dreaming up a business name. Only a few weeks later, I launched my firm. From day one, I gave myself a time frame on how long I had to make it work and told myself that if I hadn't met my (realistic) goals by that time, I'd find a job and return to life as an employee. And, well, you guessed it – I hit the goals and remain in business today!

When making what feels like a significant decision in life, it is important to step back, remove the detail and really ask yourself what is the worst that can happen if your plan does not work out. If the answer to the question does not involve putting yourself into financial distress or breaking any rules, it is likely that the worst that can happen will not actually have a detrimental or material impact on your life as a whole. It might be a bump in the road but it's unlikely to be something that you cannot recover from.

2. IF NOT NOW, THEN WHEN?

If you're anything like me, you want things to be perfect before calling them done. However, when it comes to life in business, there is never the perfect time to do anything. You will never feel like you are ready, like you have enough money or that you have enough time to bring your dream to fruition. But living in that mindset only guarantees one thing – that you will not propel yourself forward to be bigger and better than you are today.

At the time of launching my law firm, our world was in the midst of a pandemic, my first child was only five months old and I was in the process of being diagnosed with what I now know is a chronic illness – multiple sclerosis. All of those factors, separately and together, meant my life would never be the same again. The timing of my business was somewhat unexpected. I was returning from parental leave and hadn't budgeted to start a new business, nor did I have all of the right equipment in place. I didn't let that hold me back.

Whilst I had a desire to do something different, I knew that if I returned to what was comfortable, I'd never let that desire become a reality. I'd just put it off until the time was 'right'. But actually, the time is never right.

The only way that you can propel yourself forward to be bigger and better than you are today is to get started. Do something to start. Just take the first step. For me, that meant deciding on a business name, registering my company and getting minimal infrastructure in place to enable me to start work as soon as I could. The rest just had to follow.

As time passed and my business grew, I was able to add to the infrastructure, improve on the systems and processes, and really start to build the business in meaningful way.

If you wait until the perfect time to take your next leap of faith, you can be assured that the time will not come. You will always find a roadblock in your way. So, when thinking about your goals and when to really take the leap toward achieving them, ask yourself, *If not now, then when?*

3. FIND YOUR TRIBE

The journey of a solopreneur can be isolating and lonely. Whilst solopreneurs might have the support of their nearest and dearest, it is often the case that those loved ones do not fully appreciate the ins and outs of your business, your particular industry or the challenges you face – both *in* your business and *for* your business.

To make sure you have somewhere to turn on the hard days and to give yourself access to a brains trust who will listen to – and genuinely understand – your ideas, challenges and wins, you need to find your tribe.

As an early career lawyer, I often felt like I didn't quite fit in. I didn't 'walk the walk' or 'talk the talk'. I didn't want to play the corporate games and I certainly couldn't afford the fancy suits. I wanted to engage with my career, clients and colleagues on a meaningful rather than superficial level. I wanted to know my clients as people rather than a file number. I wanted to be confident that the advice I was providing to my clients was actually making a difference to their lives and not just affecting their pocket. I wanted to deliver legal services in a way that was not quite within the traditional law firm model. For many years, rather than let these desires inspire me to do something different, they created a mind-set of wondering whether a career in law was even for me. Did I have to change who I am at my core to fit into the profession? And then, something changed. Those thoughts, coupled with my desire to work differently, led me to finding the group that would fast become my tribe.

It was November 2018 and I had registered to attend a conference. By that stage of my career, I'd been to a lot of conferences. You know the ones where you get a branded pen, a bag full of brochures and you sit and stare at a stage for a few days, perhaps with some idle banter with the stranger sitting next to you? You leave with a few new ideas but an overall feeling of exhaustion. I'd heard that the conference I was going to attend was a 'conference like no other'. *I'll be the judge of that,* I thought. It turned out that what I heard was right. The conference was filled with predominantly female professionals who were all making a difference, working differently, enjoying their work, and most of all, supporting others. Finally, I'd found my tribe.

I've been to that particular conference every year since 2018 and have also joined what I will call a 'sub-group' of professionals, who are also regular attendees at that conference, in a formal networking group. Regularly in the sub-group, we share ideas, challenges and wins, and support each other through the roller-coaster ride that is small business.

Without that group of professionals, I would not have had the confidence or courage to pivot to where I am today, or to acknowledge my challenges but then to find resilience and continue to work towards my goals. My tribe have been the people who have believed in me during the times when I have been filled with self-doubt and uncertainty.

Find your tribe. Your people. The ones that get you and your business, and that you are comfortable with. They may not be in your industry, but they need to understand your realities. You also may not find them right away but keep looking. They are out there.

4. BE PURPOSEFUL

As business owners and entrepreneurs, we have a strong desire to continue moving forward towards our goals. However, it is very easy to get distracted by the latest technology, the latest trends and what your peers or competitors are doing. That is particularly so in small business when you often feel like you are working hard for very little gain. Oftentimes, we get distracted and lose focus. And then it just feels like we are on the hamster wheel.

Being purposeful about your decisions and how you spend your time in your business is one of the secrets to overcoming distractions. You will always feel like someone else is moving faster or doing better than you. Keep in mind that is only what you see on the outside. Don't compare yourself to anyone else. You don't know what is going on behind their closed doors – nor do you need to worry about that.

When making the decision to pivot, make a list of the tasks you want to achieve. Write it down on paper. There is something special about a tangible to-do list!

The tasks on your list might relate to marketing, systems and processes, recruitment or general administration. My tip is to make sure that the tasks are meaningful, purposeful activities. Avoid any ambiguity! Be as clear as possible about what it is that you need to get done.

As you write down your tasks, either as a conscious effort to write a list or a brain dump as tasks pop into your mind, keep your purpose, values and goals front of mind. This will help you to determine whether the task you think you need to do is going to get you to where you want to go. Are you doing the task for you or for someone else?

Once you know the tasks you want to achieve, put them in order of most important to least important, or 'must do' tasks and 'one day' tasks. This will help you to prioritise where to spend your energy and know what tasks are less urgent and can wait until you have some downtime.

As you embark on your pivot towards success, work through your list. Be purposeful about how you spend your time and the order in which you complete your tasks. Chip away at the 'one day' tasks when you have some downtime or need a creative outlet. Importantly, when a task is done, cross it off the list. That will give you a sense of achievement, and over time, as each item on the list is crossed off, you'll see how much you have accomplished!

I keep a book with a golden cover on my desk. Whenever I have an idea about something I could or should do, in business or in life, I jot it down in the book. Some tasks sit on the pages for weeks and months and others are completed almost immediately. Either way, I know what has to be done, I am purposeful about prioritising and working through the list and I get a sense of achievement when each task is completed. The list also serves as a good reminder of how far I've come and what my thought patterns have been over time. There are even some items on the list that will never get done because my priorities or focus have shifted. And that's okay.

Imposter syndrome is rife in small business owners and particularly women. Sure, we can take inspiration and motivation from what others are doing but don't compare yourself to those people. I have no doubt they also have a list of tasks to work through over time – and it might just be that they've had more time to work through their list than you have had to work through yours!

5. START SMALL BUT DREAM BIG

Pivoting into a new phase of your career or a new business venture is filled with a roller-coaster of emotions. Your new chapter might be something you have dreamt about for a long time or, like me, it might be an opportunity that comes along somewhat unexpectedly with little time to plan.

No matter how your pivot comes about, you need to remember that nothing worth having comes quickly or easily. As the saying goes, *'Rome wasn't built in a day.'* Start small, but dream big.

From the time I made the decision to launch my new law firm to the date that it launched was just three short weeks. With the help of a friend, we worked out the bare minimum that was required for me to kick off. Anything more than that was a bonus. For me, the bare minimum was a computer, my mobile phone, appropriate insurances and licences, a business name and a bank account. Everything else could come later!

By the date that I celebrated the first anniversary of the launch of my business, I'd purchased more equipment for the business, improved my website and branding, purchased subscription software to help me with the day-to-day operation of the business and employed some team members. None of that was needed when I started out. However, it's part of my bigger dream to grow the business and a step in the right direction towards making that dream a reality.

I started small but continue to dream big. That dream will continue to evolve but knowing that I am carefully building a strong foundation without rushing in is going to be one of the secrets to the success of my business.

***

So, there we have it. By asking yourself some simple questions, surrounding yourself with the right group of people, staying focused on where you're going but still having the imagination to dream big, you will find the confidence to pivot.

SARAH STODDART

Sarah Stoddart is the founder and sole director of Vitality Law Australia, a boutique law firm based on Brisbane which provides small and medium business owners across Australia with clear pathways and peace of mind to grow their health care businesses.

In November 2020, in the midst of a pandemic and shortly after the birth of her first child, Sarah launched her law firm. The firm was borne as a result of her strong desire to work flexibly and to practice law differently. Whilst she enjoyed the practice of law, Sarah didn't want to work long hours or spend time commuting – both of which would take her away from enjoying her family and being present to witness their important milestones and achievements. Rather than settle back into the security that her role at the time provided, she decided to take a leap of faith, forge her own path in law and open her own law firm. Needless to say, she hasn't looked back.

Ten years earlier, Sarah had commenced her legal career as a graduate lawyer at an international law firm, before moving into an in-house role and then into boutique law firms. By age thirty, she was a law firm director.

Sarah is recognised as a leader in the health care industry and is one of only a few lawyers in Australia with specialist experience working with pharmacy businesses. Whilst her focus is on pharmacy businesses, she also assists dentists, physiotherapists and medical centre owners with their business needs.

Sarah has extensive experience with the sale and purchase of health care businesses, as well as applications to regulatory bodies for approval of new health care businesses. In addition to her focus on health care businesses, Sarah is also highly skilled in general commercial matters, employment law and conveyancing.

Sarah works closely with her clients to understand their business, provide them with education about issues relevant to their industry and to help them achieve business and professional growth. She regularly speaks at conferences, delivers workplace training and offers guidance on issues facing business owners via free blog posts.

Clients describe Sarah as friendly, approachable and efficient. She is the driver behind Vitality Law Australia delivering legal services differently and in a way that is more simplistic but more easily understood by her clients. She understands the demands of life in small business, particularly with a growing family, and is genuinely interested in building and fostering strong relationships, and helping her clients succeed.

In November 2021, Sarah was named as the *Lawyers Weekly* Australian Women in Law Sole Practitioner of the Year. That award recognises outstanding performance by an individual who has chosen to roll out their own practice. She was also a finalist in the AusMumpreneur Business Awards in the categories of Disabled Business Excellence and Emerging AusMumpreneur. The category of Disabled Business Excellence is recognition of Sarah's achievements in business despite being unexpectedly diagnosed with multiple sclerosis only three months after her law firm commenced practice.

As well as running Vitality Law Australia, Sarah is an adjunct lecturer at the College of Law Queensland, regularly contributes articles to the *Australian Journal of Pharmacy* and *Lawyers Weekly*, and is a past board director and chair of the governance subcommittee of the Queensland Alliance for Mental Health.

Website: vitalitylawaustralia.com

SELF-CARE & SELF-COMPASSION

Dr Vanessa Atienza-Hipolito

When I had my second child ten years ago, I was four dress sizes over-weight! I felt yucky! I kept saying to myself, *It's okay because you just had a baby, just finished your fellowship training and studying for exams to be a qualified radiologist here in Australia and you are breastfeeding and caring for two kids now.* Honestly, I miss my OLD self. I used to play tennis and go for long walks on the weekends before having kids. I decided, at that moment, that enough is enough. It was time for me to take care of ME so I could be a better person within. I strongly believe that I am a better mother and wife if I am feeling great within. I chose to prioritise ME time! I am so grateful for my husband Glenn and our family who supported me and helped me look after my kids while I made time for MYSELF.

For me, the only skill that matters is MINDSET. Decision-making, building my mental stamina and training my mind. I believe that you can train your mind like training your muscles. I need to have the ability to learn and train my mind to take action and move forward. It is the only way forward towards my small goals, bigger goals and dreams.

Ever since, my mantra which is saved on my iPhone home screen is: *'Today, I choose to be the best version of myself.'* This mantra has helped a lot towards my personal and professional goals and business endeavours while at the same time taking care of my young family and still enjoying life!

Self-care and self-compassion can be cultivated in several ways.

EXERCISE FOR SELF-IMPROVEMENT, SELF-CONFIDENCE AND SELF-ACCEPTANCE

In my quest to be a 1% BETTER VERSION OF MYSELF every day, I prioritised making time for exercise. I was working full-time at a private imaging facility which included driving and flying out to regional areas in Western Australia. Despite my full-on schedule, I woke up every morning to exercise thirty to sixty minutes a day consistently, make time for meal preparation and make lifestyle changes with the food I ate. I learned how to cook and prepare simple and healthy meals. I saw the transformation in myself physically, emotionally and mentally.

Ten years ago, I was not able to run for over a minute without being out of breath. I challenged myself to start running. I have found running to be my happy place. I have completed many half-marathons and marathon events since then.

Six years ago, I could not swim in the pool for more than 10m without being tired and out of breath. I was determined to learn how to swim to overcome my panic attacks in the ocean. I hired a coached and made time for swimming lessons and swim practice. Since then, I have been swimming regularly in the pool and once a week in the ocean – all year round. I have completed many endurance swim events in the ocean and half-ironman races. I am in my happy place every time I swim in the ocean. It is the place where I switch off and just enjoy the moment. I make time to swim in my happy place every Sunday morning. My favourite swim time is during sunrise when I see the sun rising on the horizon while I breathe from side to side. It is my magical place! It is my magic moment!

I celebrate my mini-wins and mini-milestones. I celebrate myself for even making time for ME time!

I do not have time for exercise, but I make time. Even ten minutes of exercise every day is a celebration of MYSELF. Ten thousand steps a day are ten thousand mini-wins. A thirty-minute walk or a one-hour bike ride on weekends. A thirty-minute walk on the beach after work is my time to release, reset and recalibrate.

It is time to open your calendar and plan your weekly and monthly exercise regimen.

SELF-CARE IS SELF-LOVE. IT IS NOT SELFISHNESS. IT IS A NECESSITY

Being an entrepreneur and a specialist doctor can be very stressful. It can be emotionally, physically and mentally exhausting, especially when starting out and in the early stages of setting up, planning and building a business. During my journey, I tended to be focused on success, productivity and just trying to thrive and survive while overcoming challenges. There are many ups and downs.

Making time for exercise has been life-changing for me. It helps with my productivity at work. I learned a lot about myself. I learned that deciding to train for races, especially endurance sports, is such an achievement. Due to my work and family commitments, training with friends and clubs can be difficult to fit into my schedule. It can be a lonely journey to train alone. I learned that my strongest muscle and worst enemy is my mind. I learned and am still learning how to master my mindset. I learned that I could do anything. 'Anything is possible,' is the mantra of most ironman athletes. I learned that in any endurance sport, mindset is 90%, training is 10%. I have the choice to be critical of myself by being slow compared to my age-group athletes, but I choose self-kindness and self-compassion by forgiving myself for being slow. I stopped comparing myself to them. I stopped comparing myself those in their sixties and seventies that I cannot outswim, outrun and overtake on the bike. I am fully aware that my personal best is different from other people's PBs. I must set my own race, my own pace and my own record.

Personal goal-setting and my quest to be a better version of myself led me to dream big in my career and business. It has helped me PIVOT my profession and my business by applying the growth mindset principle.

Every day, I choose to use positive inner dialogue. I choose not to be self-critical. I do not use nasty words to myself. I train my mind not to hate myself every time I fail or make mistakes. I always acknowledge my mistakes and forgive myself.

It takes a lot of practice to develop self-love, self-respect and self-kindness. It takes a lot of patience and self-awareness to practice self-care and self-compassion by mastering a positive mindset.

During my self-discovery and mastery of self-love, I was able to pivot my personal and professional growth by making time to read and listen to audiobooks on growth mindset and personal development. I binge-watch webinars, podcasts and YouTube videos and follow business coaches on all social media platforms. Despite my busy work, I make time to listen to audiobooks or inspiring podcasts during my commute, during school pick-up and drop-off, during my drive to and from shops and especially when I do my weekly long walk-run along the beach. I invested in myself so I can be a better person, a better parent, a better wife, a better leader of my team and a better doctor. I also attend a lot of online and face-to-face meetings, workshops and conferences related to my professional field.

What I love reading now is the new book by Mel Robbins, *The High 5 Habit*. She talks about practicing the simple tool of high-fiving yourself in the mirror every day after brushing your teeth.

Starting today, I challenge you to be your inner compassion coach.

Do this daily for the next twenty-one days.
What are three things I love about myself?

1. _____

2. _____

3. _____

ACCORDING TO MY HUSBAND GLENN: 'DEFINE BUSY-NESS?!' THERE IS A DIFFERENCE BETWEEN BEING BUSY AND BEING PRODUCTIVE

People ask me every day, 'How was your day?' or, 'How was your week?' or, 'How are you?'

Before, I used to tell them, 'I was crazy busy!' or, 'It was madness!' or, 'It was toxic!'

I have changed my language now. I think there is a negative connotation around saying, 'I am busy.' It is sometimes coined 'addicted to work' or 'workaholism'.

Now, whenever people ask me how I am, I always tell them, 'I was productive!' or, 'I had a very productive day [or week].'

It is always a great day to be productive! I know that I can do anything, but I cannot do *everything*. **Time management and planning** our daily and weekly tasks and activities are important for me and my family. I am always inspired by the *High Performance Habits* book and I use the planner, both by Brendon Burchard.

I prioritise my non-negotiables, which are now my learned habits, and I am still a work in progress:

- I always prioritise and make time for my family by spending quality time with them. I always maximise the use of my calendar and journal. I make sure that my family activities and quality time with them are marked in my already full-on day calendar.

- I calendar all my future goals with the date and year. I love my affirmations and vision board! I use this for my manifestation by posting my big goals and dreams.
- Nearly every morning when I wake up, I write in my journal. I always first write down a list of what I am grateful for in my life.
- I practice self-awareness so that when I am burnt-out, I know I can always say NO to things that are not important in that moment. I set personal boundaries. I make time for ME to reset and recalibrate.
- I am proactive in organising weekly coffee catch-up chats or monthly catch-up dinners and drinks with my friends.
- I win my day if I meditate first thing in the morning when I wake up even for just five to fifteen minutes.
- I always try to apply the positive mind shift principle in any challenges and obstacles I encounter in my daily life.

Win your day by daily regular planning.

ENHANCE SELF-LOVE THROUGH MUSIC TO SELF-REGULATE

Music is a part of our human life. It is one of the universal languages that exists in cultures all over the world.

Music entertains us when we are stuck in traffic during rush hour, during school pick-up and drop-off, during the long drive when we go on holiday or while waiting in the queue at the shops. It motivates us when we are at the gym or doing any exercise while walking, running, attending Pilates or yoga classes.

Music increases our dopamine levels – the 'feel-good' hormone. It prompts us to savour the moment if we listen to uplifting music. I often listen to music when doing a guided meditation.

Music helps us to self-regulate when we are under stress or broken-hearted. It affects our emotions, it can make us happy or sad or nostalgic.

Tips on using music for self-care:

1. Create a playlist that makes you happy, positive and motivated. You can use music to give yourself a boost when you are feeling down. I admit that I am a karaoke queen! My all-time favourite karaoke songs are:
   - *I Will Survive* by Gloria Gaynor
   - *Dancing Queen* by ABBA

   My favourite running/motivational songs:
   - *Fight Song* by Rachel Platten
   - *Stronger* by Kelly Clarkson

2. Create a playlist of songs with a slow tempo. At work, I always have relaxation or meditation music on while I perform breast procedures. I cannot work on a patient without music. This kind of music also helps my patients calm down and relax.

3. Use music for self-care if you are overwhelmed or undergoing challenges and difficult emotions. My mother used to tell me that music is the highest form of prayer. My singing at church helps me feel grounded and connects me to my spirituality. I use music for self-care often at the end of the week. In my busy life as a doctor and business owner, I always prioritise my singing in the choir. Friday night is my favourite day of the week because it is our weekly choir practice, and we have been doing this for the past ten years. I love to belt out all the stress of the week. I sing in the church choir three times a month with my husband Glenn who is our choirmaster and accompanist playing the keyboard or piano. It also allows me to give praise and thanks for all my blessings. It binds our family and our community.

4. Music is a skill that can be learned – just like learning to drive. I have loved to sing and dance since I was a kid. I love listening to music. Music has been part of my life from growing up and in my and my family's daily life. I love going out with girlfriends to dance at

concerts and music shows. You do not need to be a musician to sing, play or appreciate music. I am giving you full permission to sing in the shower. You could even join a community choir. You are never too old to learn a musical instrument too. Just sing or dance – or both – like no-one is watching and have fun and LIVE!

Self-love, growth mindset, exercise and music helped me to be a healthier version of myself, to have a work-life balance. I am UNSTOPPABLE!

As a full-time working mother with never-ending house chores, a long to-do list, a long list of clutter to declutter and an entrepreneur, I do not have time to get sick. I do not know where in my calendar I can fit in my health checks. Most of the time, I feel that I am a Wonder Woman with superhuman powers who will never get sick.

As a health advocate, I would like to not only reiterate the importance of nutrition and fitness for overall health and wellbeing but also promote the importance of regular medical checks.

MY HEALTH IS MY MOST IMPORTANT ASSET! MY HEALTH IS MY INVESTMENT

To protect my health investment, I make time for important preventive medical health checks.

The goal of preventive medicine is to protect, promote and maintain health and wellbeing and prevent illness, disease, disability and early death.

Based on the statistics of the National Breast Cancer Foundation:

- One in seven women and one in seven hundred men will be diagnosed with breast cancer in their lifetime.
- In 2021, to date, over 3,138 Australians have passed away from breast cancer.
- On average, nine Australians die every day from breast cancer.

As a specialist breast radiologist, it is my mission to educate and empower women **to be in charge of their health**. Currently, there is a knowledge gap in breast health and imaging awareness. A woman diagnosed with breast cancer has a better chance of surviving the disease if detected early by imaging: a mammogram, breast ultrasound or both. I advise women to regularly book an appointment for their breast tests before they can feel a lump and before their doctor can feel it. She should not need to wait until she is fifty years old to get a mammogram. Women should not wait for a change, a lump or symptoms in their breasts. While more people are being diagnosed with breast cancer each year, thanks to improved screening techniques and treatments, fewer people are dying.

To all mums, aunties, grandmothers, besties, colleagues and women in your community, I am encouraging you to make time to see your doctor for your routine clinical breast examination, book your mammogram appointment and discuss the need for a supplementary breast ultrasound check.

To the men, I encourage you to lovingly prompt the special women in your life to make time and prioritise their breast health check and imaging tests.

Here is my THINGS TO DO FOR *ME* list:

- Annual health check with my doctor which includes blood tests.
- Breast and gynaecological check.
- Dental and optical check.
- Monthly beauty appointments which include: hair care, waxing and manicure and pedicure.

The fact that you have finished reading this chapter, I celebrate you for the beginning of your journey towards self-love … to be a 1% better version of yourself. Imagine what you could be in one year … a 365% better version of yourself! Your awesome SELF will love YOU!

PLEASE SAY THIS OUT LOUD EVERY DAY:

Today, I prioritise self-kindness.

Today, I prioritise MYSELF.

Today, I prioritise ME time.

Today, I celebrate MYSELF.

Today, I am cheering MYSELF.

Today, I appreciate MYSELF.

Today, I appreciate ME.

Today, I prioritise my self-love, my own joy and happiness to be able to give more love, joy and happiness to others.

Today, I prioritise taking care of my health, mind and body.

Today, I will surround myself with loving people who will uplift and encourage me.

Today, I will ask for help whenever I need it.

I am a better person today than yesterday.

My prayer for you is:
Let all that you do be done in LOVE.
(1 Corinthians 16:14)

DR VANESSA ATIENZA-HIPOLITO

Dr Vanessa Atienza-Hipolito MD FRANZCR is a specialist radiologist with subspecialty interests in breast imaging and intervention, musculoskeletal imaging, interventional and vascular radiology and paediatric radiology. She leads the team at Women's and Breast Imaging (WBI) in Cottesloe, Western Australia, as a business owner and clinical director. WBI is a forty-one-year-old business which she took over in 2014. It is a boutique breast imaging centre based in a heritage-listed building, the only private imaging centre in Western Australia which offers a one-stop-shop dedicated to screening and diagnosis of breast diseases in women, but also including paediatrics and men. This centre is a leading provider of the latest technology in mammography to improve early detection of cancer which includes (Volpara) advanced breast density measurement and digital breast tomosynthesis.

WBI services offer all imaging and image-guided biopsy modalities relating to the breast (except MRI): mammogram (3D-breast tomosynthesis), breast ultrasound, core biopsy, vacuum-assisted core biopsy and excision, fine needle aspiration biopsy (FNA), ultrasound-guided abscess and cyst drainage, breast implant assessment and surveillance, and gynaecological ultrasound.

In addition, she provides teleradiology reporting for Ultrasound Services which provides general ultrasound service for local and remote WA in Mandurah, Applecross, Harvey and Armadale.

Dr Vanessa is committed and passionate about clinical teaching and mentoring junior doctors and medical students. She is an adjunct clinical senior lecturer, clinical supervisor, OSCE examiner and clinician-student mentor at the Curtin Medical School, Curtin University, and adjunct clinical senior lecturer and clinical supervisor at University of Western Australia.

She worked for BreastScreen WA Bunbury Assessment Clinic as lead breast radiologist and as a screen-reader at BreastScreen WA East Perth head office from 2014 to March 2017.

Dr Vanessa was named AusMumpreneur 2021 in the following categories:

People's Choice Awards – Making a Difference (Local Community) Gold Award Winner

Health and Wellbeing Business Silver Award Winner

She was also named as finalist for the 2021 AusMumpreneur Awards in the following categories:

AusMumpreneur of the Year Award

Business Excellence Award

Women's Champion Award

In June 2019, Dr Vanessa was awarded the Millennial Achiever Award presented by Filipino Australian Club of Perth Inc (FACPI) during the Philippines Independence Day Gala Night at The Crown Towers, Perth, WA.

She is married with a son and daughter and contributes actively to her community in numerous ways by providing pro bono health education, ensuring they have access to current information on optimal care for breast health and the best available breast imaging technology. It is her passion to help women and raise awareness on the importance of breast checks and early breast cancer detection. She is an advocate of preventive medicine. As a founding member of The Brilliant Foundation, she has published two articles to share her knowledge and expertise, highlighting the importance of preventive medicine in breast health.

She is a great supporter of medical research through personal fund-raising and carries out clinical research in her own field. She has presented in numerous local and international medical conferences. The highlight of her career was when she was invited to be a speaker and faculty in the 105th Scientific Assembly and Annual Meeting, Radiological Society of North America (RSNA) in Chicago, USA, in December 2019. The topic of her presentation was Breast Imaging in Western Australia: How we do it in the Land Down Under, A Case-based Review of the Breast (Interactive Session).

On her spare time, she loves singing in her church choir, triathlon, swimming in the ocean, running, cycling, playing tennis, playing Scrabble with the family and travelling. The highlights of her travels were when she completed half-marathon races in Budapest, Hungary, and Bordeaux, France. She is eager to do more 'run-cations' in the future.

Website: wbi.net.au

SELF-CARE

Listening to yourself & doing what
makes you happy
Vanessa Marrama

This chapter is all about defining what self-care is/can be and how you can start to incorporate some of it into your life. It is here to serve as a reminder of why listening to yourself is so important and the profound benefits it can have on you personally and professionally.

WHAT DOES SELF-CARE MEAN TO YOU?

What is self-care, anyway?

The World Health Organization defines self-care as, 'The ability of individuals, families and communities to promote health, prevent disease, maintain health and to cope with illness and disability with or without the support of a health care provider.'

When I read this definition, the first two words I notice are: *promote* and *prevent*. Promote amongst those around you and prevent ill health within you.

I then concentrate on my mental, spiritual and emotional health. Why? Because 1) I have no issue with regular exercise so my physical

239

health is covered, and 2) I am an ambitious woman who is juggling so much in her life at any given time that the first thing impacted when trying to juggle everything is my mental, spiritual and emotional health.

But it's okay because, like you, I am resilient and courageous and I have (more on that below!) the insight to acknowledge the challenges and the associated health effects that come with **choosing** to live a busy life.

If living a busy life is something that you have chosen to do, then own it: identify and acknowledge the areas of your health that are being impacted by your busy lifestyle and slowly do something about it. Listen and acknowledge the exhausted, frustrated and overwhelmed thoughts you are having! They are totally natural and okay to have, believe me.

I have always been an ambitious woman. I started working when I was fourteen and nine months, and I have worked ever since. My work increased dramatically after having my two boys, and since then, my life has revolved around paid and unpaid (parenting) work. I never appreciated how many hours there were in a day until I became a parent and started my own business.

I was deeply affected by the change in my life. I suffered postnatal depression (twice!). I was numb, miserable, ashamed and confused but I finally plucked up the courage to do something about it.

I knew that if I didn't, then no-one could. I let go of the guilt, shame and the feelings of failure and stopped comparing myself to other mums. I did, however, seek help.

I remember the first phone call. I remember speaking to the counsellor and she validated everything I shared. In those moments, I knew that it was all going to be okay. I also knew that if I didn't continue this confronting and difficult journey, I would only let myself and my innocent children down, so I continued on and booked my next appointment.

This is what self-care is about: acknowledging when things aren't quite right and then doing something (**whatever is right for you**) about it so that you can be the best version of you.

How you can do this is to follow.

ACKNOWLEDGING YOUR INNER VOICE AMONGST ALL THE NOISE

Noticing and acting on your inner voice.

'You can think of your inner voice almost like your highest self,' explains professional intuitive and author of *Self-Care for Empaths,* Tanya Carroll Richardson. 'It's that wise part of you that can float high above the details of the moment, your own emotions, and the emotions of others to get an eagle-eye, more objective perspective on a situation.'

To be able to acknowledge, and therefore act on, what your inner voice is telling you, you need to allow yourself the time and space to do so. I acknowledge, however, that this may be easier said (or written!) than done because you are so used to either putting the needs and wants of others before your own and/or you are living such a busy life juggling so many things that you don't have the time or energy to tune in to yourself and your inner voice. Cooking dinner, checking your emails or taking the washing out seems far more appealing and easier to do than taking a moment or two to listen to *you,* the person who knows you best.

These destructive habits need to end! You need to give yourself the time and space to stop, acknowledge and act on what your inner voice is telling you. I know it's easier said than done and it will take plenty of failed attempts to get there, but when you do, I promise that it will be so worth it.

You will realise that putting aside a few minutes at a time to stop and listen to your inner voice is all you need and it isn't that hard. The world around you can, in fact, survive without you during that time. Doing this more and more, and perhaps even lengthening those initial few minutes to a duration that is practical and even more beneficial to you, will help enable you to live and show up in life as the best version of you.

As astrologer and author of *Cosmic Health,* Jennifer Racioppi, says: 'It will help you fully discern your wisdom, guidance and direction, and there's nothing more potent or powerful than trusting yourself and confidently following your truth.'

I had a conversation with the father of my children one day and I told him that I wanted to make time for myself. My inner voice was screaming at me to do so. I kept ignoring it. Drowning it out with work, kids, chores etc. But I paid the price because I had reached a stage of utter exhaustion, unhappiness and just *blah!*

As expected, he was totally supportive of me, so I started doing the things I enjoy. I would get my nails done, do some colouring-in, read a book, go for a walk or sit outside in the backyard with nature, start my own business – whatever I felt like doing, and I let my inner voice decide.

Sometimes, all I needed was a couple of minutes to just pause and take a few deep breaths. At that moment, I listened to myself and acted.

I struggled, however, to keep it consistent because, at times, I would ignore my inner voice and just keep doing what I was doing on autopilot, and that is where I made the mistake, because I was tending to other people's needs and their self-care/wants rather than listening to my inner alarm bell and dedicating that time to myself and my own self-care/wants.

Don't get me wrong: it's hard for me to put myself first, and at times, I slip up (and that's totally fine!) but overall, I am learning to stop and listen to my inner voice and do what's right for me so I can be the best self-cared (and self-loved) version of me possible.

PUTTING A SMILE ON YOUR DIAL

Life is too short not to be happy.

Happiness is an emotional state characterised by feelings of joy, satisfaction, contentment and fulfillment. While happiness has many different definitions, it is often described as involving positive emotions and life satisfaction (verywellmind.com 2020).

Now that we know what happiness is, it's time to feel it, experience and treasure it. One way to do this is by smiling.

According to Walden University, smiling helps you feel better because it increases mood-enhancing hormones while decreasing stress-enhancing hormones. It also reduces overall blood pressure. And because you typically smile when you're happy, the muscles used to smile trigger your brain to produce more endorphins – the chemical that relieves pain and stress.
But it's important to acknowledge that not all smiles mean that you are happy, so the smile I, and I'm sure others around you, want you to display, is one of true and utter happiness.

How? Well, this is where listening to yourself comes in.

WHY LISTENING TO YOURSELF IS SO IMPORTANT

You are the only person who knows you the best.

There is nothing worse than being told by others what they think is best for you.

You are the only person who can make those decisions and vice versa. It's okay to listen to other people's opinions and advice, but at the end of the day, the only person you need to be accountable to is yourself.

Listening to yourself:
- *Is empowering* because you are taking a stand and acknowledging how you feel. Once you do it, you will notice that your posture will improve, you will take a bigger and deeper breath in and you will smile an authentic smile because you have momentarily listened to yourself and put yourself first.
- *Is invigorating* because you are finally able to let go of the guilt, the *I don't deserve to put aside time for myself* thoughts and you feel invigorated because of it.
- *Isn't as scary as it seems.* We are our own worst enemy. We think that

if we do something for us, 'bad' things are going to happen. I.e. the kids will cry for me or there will be a client emergency. The reality is that these are just your thoughts, and as long as the kids are looked after and your client isn't in a life-or-death situation (which I highly doubt), then these things can and will wait! Gosh – you may even find that when you do get back home or back to your desk that all you have waiting for you is happy kids and/or an inbox with a handful of emails and no SOS texts!

- *Is self-preservation in action* because you are listening to yourself and acting on those thoughts, which in turn, helps you to become an even better human to be around, and who knows, you may even live longer and feel better in the process.
- *Is letting go of the weight of the world.* You can't and shouldn't be expected to be all things to everyone. It's not humanly possible, so let that expectation go (if you have it) and allow yourself the opportunity and freedom to put yourself and your needs first. I promise that others do the same!
- *Is the best way to live (and lead) by example* because it's showing other women out there that it can be done. Many of us feel a sense of guilt or unworthiness when we want to put ourselves first but that shouldn't be the case because you are just as human as anyone else, and therefore, you deserve to put yourself and your needs first.

As you continue to put yourself first and the benefits of this split second of selfishness start to shine through, you then start to become a role model for your children, family, friends and wider community, and how inspiring is that? You are a living, breathing example of what can be achieved if you only listen to yourself and your needs and act on them. It's not rocket science, but it can be just as hard.

I was unhappy in my relationship. I was 'with' a wonderful man who only wanted to take care of and support me. I settled, because up until meeting him, I had met the wrong men. He was different, nice and safe, but (there's always a but!) my inner voice wouldn't be silenced.

It was telling me to act because I was unhappy. I had this man who was my soulmate, my protector, the father of my children, but something was off – I just didn't have that spark, that fire in me, when I was in his company.

I soon realised that I had to do something about it, but it took me two years and two kids later to act. I moved out with the kids and took some time for myself. We started relationship counselling so we could figure out the new reality and I laid it all out on the table, as did he.

They were hard conversations to have but they were finally said, and it felt good to finally acknowledge my feelings, be heard, and most importantly, not have an inner voice screaming at me!

Now, we are back to living under the same roof as best friends and co-parents to our two very cheeky boys who we are trying to raise as best we can.

SELF-CARE IN A PROFESSIONAL WORLD

*Do what you love, the way you want, with people you want
to do it with.*

After I became a mum, I listened to my inner voice and started my own business from home. I became a virtual assistant (VA). I started my own business because I wanted more in my life. I wanted a sense of achievement, accomplishment, a professional challenge and a degree of financial independence. It was a tough hard road for the first year or two while I found my feet, but I was happy. I had something that was mine from the very beginning and something that gave me a purpose, a challenge and an opportunity to interact with other working professionals.

Don't get me wrong: being a mum is great and I can't tell you how many times I have watched kids' cartoons on repeat, but working is in my blood – it helps shape who I am as a woman and I needed to reawaken that part of my life again, so I did.

Now, five years later, I am an online business manager (OBM) and I have a team of VAs who are mostly mums and they are supporting me with my clients, who are also mums. I have joined forces with a local charity which is dedicated to supporting women who want to re-enter the workforce. These women come from a range of backgrounds and circumstances and they are in need of support so that they can feel empowered to be the best version of themselves possible.

My goal, my *why*, my what makes me happy and what fills my self-care cup: to build a community of working mums who are supporting other working mums.

Why am I sharing this? Because I want to demonstrate the power of your inner voice. The person inside you who knows you best, who can guide you in the direction you need and deserve to go. The person who can help you achieve professional satisfaction and happiness in whatever way it looks for you.

OVERVIEW

Self-care is about preventing ill health and promoting good health. How you can start to do this is by noticing and listening to your inner voice. Once you do this, you will naturally begin to incorporate self-care into your life so that you can smile even more to achieve even greater happiness in whatever way it looks for you, both in your personal and professional life.

VANESSA MARRAMA

Vanessa is a mum to two boys and a small business owner. She has a master's in business administration and over ten years' management experience. She has applied those skills and experiences to starting her own online business (Vanessa M Taking Care of Business) offering online business management (OBM) and virtual assistant (VA) services to other like-minded mums and women in business.

Vanessa mostly recruits the services of VAs who are also mums so that they have an opportunity to apply and develop their skills and experiences within their relevant industry. Vanessa is determined to empower and support her team of VAs so that they become successful mumpreneurs in their own right.

Vanessa is passionate about giving back to the community so that other like-minded mums and women in business feel empowered and supported to succeed in whatever career path they choose and that is why she has partnered with a small charity, Dress for Success South East Melbourne, to do just that!

ABOUT PEACE & KATY AND SPEAKING OPPORTUNITIES

Peace and Katy are the dynamic duo behind AusMumpreneur, Australia's number one community for mums in business; The Women's Business School, providing dedicated education for aspiring and established female founders; and Women Changing the World Press, amplifying the voices of thought leaders, female founders and women changing the world.

Peace Mitchell is a TEDx speaker, international keynote speaker, retreat facilitator and workshop presenter.

If you want your audience to be captivated by a heart-centred, warm and engaging thought leader and speaker then look no further.

With experience delivering keynote presentations on connection, business success, magic and productivity, there's nothing Peace loves more than engaging with your delegates to make your event a huge success.

If you've got an online or in-person event coming up and want to create a magical, warm and engaging atmosphere, please get in touch.

peace@womensbusinesscollective.com
+61 431 615 107

ABOUT THE WOMEN'S BUSINESS SCHOOL

The Women's Business School is a business school designed exclusively for women. Providing opportunities for innovative female founders to scale their startup, connect with fellow founders and gain advice and guidance from successful entrepreneurs and experts. Through the award-winning Incubator and Accelerator programs, founders receive world-class entrepreneurial education from a team of high-level experts and entrepreneurs as well as mentoring, advice and access to successful female entrepreneurs across a range of industries. If you're ready to take your business to the next level, apply today!

thewomensbusinessschool.com

ABOUT AUSMUMPRENEUR

Australia's number one community for Mumpreneurs. The Aus-Mumpreneur Awards are a national event recognising and celebrating Australia's best and brightest mums in business. Held annually, these awards recognise the incredible women who are balancing business and motherhood and creating innovative, high-quality and remarkable brands across a range of industries.

ausmumpreneur.com

ABOUT WOMEN CHANGING THE WORLD PRESS

Women Changing the World press publishes thought leaders, female founders and women who are committed to making the world a better place through their words and actions. We believe that investing in women is the most powerful way to change the world and we are passionate about amplifying women's voices, stories and ideas and providing more opportunities for women to share their message with the world. If you have a story that the world needs to hear, get in touch today.

wcwpress.com

www.ingramcontent.com/pod-product-compliance
Lightning Source LLC
Chambersburg PA
CBHW030500210326
41597CB00013B/733